Rembrandt Peale

GEORGE WASHINGTON

GEORGE WASHINGTON

by

THORA THORSMARK

SCOTT, FORESMAN AND COMPANY
CHICAGO   ATLANTA   DALLAS   NEW YORK

TO THE READER

"It will be the duty of the historian and the sage, in all ages, to omit no occasion of commemorating the immortal name of Washington." So spoke a famous British educator in the year 1860. Some of us may never before have seen these words, but their spirit lives in the heart of every American. The year 1932 is bringing with it many memorials in celebration of the bicentennial of George Washington's birth. It is hoped that this volume may have a part among these memorials, in presenting a side of Washington that is sometimes lost sight of in the brilliant light of his military achievements. In the pages that follow, the author considers especially the personal characteristics that made George Washington the outstanding figure in a generation of great men.

Much of the material presented here has been drawn from sources such as the following: biographical studies by early writers, chief among whom are Dr. Jared Sparks and Dr. Benson J. Lossing, who had the advantage of contact with the generation of those who knew the living Washington; the *Memoirs of Washington,* by George Washington Parke Custis, grandson of Martha Washington; the diary of Washington's secretary, Colonel Tobias Lear; and letters of Washington himself, each one of which reveals some essential quality of personality that eludes the mere biographical record.

Throughout the volume the author has endeavored so to combine and supplement the letters, memoirs, and biographical studies that the pages will present a unified narrative. The earlier chapters introduce the Virginia youth who faces warring Indians and French with coolness, but who blushes and stammers when publicly congratulated by his friends. Chapters three and four present the thoughtful citizen, taking part in the legislative councils of the colony of Virginia, and thrilling to the eloquence of Patrick Henry. From the thoughtful citizen, who has deliberated much with men like Mason, Randolph, and Franklin, emerges, in later pages, the daring "rebel," selected by his countrymen as commander-in-chief of the Colonial forces. The conflict ended, the victorious military leader next appears as a dominant influence among those chosen to form a responsible government. Then, as president of the new republic, the statesman is shown laboring to realize his ideal of thirteen states working harmoniously under a strong central government.

Washington is last seen at Mount Vernon. Here he receives a succession of military friends, statesmen, and foreign visitors of prominence, who have come to renew old associations, to take counsel, or simply to salute the man of whom a great historian once wrote, "No nobler figure ever stood in the forefront of a nation's life."

Much has been said by his countrymen in praise of Washington, but appreciation of his greatness is not limited to Americans. A brief chapter of estimates, by men of other lands, closes the volume.

CONTENTS

WASHINGTON'S BIRTHPLACE AT WAKEFIELD

CHAPTER I

THE WASHINGTON FAMILY

Warriors and kings the world over have proclaimed the military genius of George Washington.

It is the privilege of the American citizen not only to commemorate this military genius, which won the acclaim of the world, but also to perpetuate the personal qualities which made Washington an outstanding figure in a generation of men of the highest attainments.

The English forbears of George Washington were early heard of in the colony of Virginia. A Colonel Ball, his maternal great grandfather, there served the British king in company with a Colonel Washington. As officers of the colonial army it was their duty to punish the depredations of hostile Indians and to suppress the rebellion fomented by the fiery Bacon. A scant century later the martial proclivities of these two modest Virginia colonels were fused in the being whose passion for liberty attained for his country the justice which Bacon sought with such tragic results.

Little is known of the Ball family in England, except that they were members of the landed gentry, worthy people of little prominence.

From the year 1183 the name of De Wessyngton figures conspicuously in the records of church and state. Washington Irving relates that a William Weshington, of Weshington, was taken prisoner in the battle of

Lewes, in 1264. In 1538 a Laurence Washington purchased from Henry the Eighth the manor of Sulgrave in Northamptonshire. This Laurence Washington was at one time mayor of Northampton, and it is from him that the Virginia Washingtons are descended. In the next century we read of a Sir Henry Washington, a nephew of the Duke of Buckingham, and his devoted loyalty to King Charles the First. Cromwell had driven Charles into hiding, and was sweeping his adherents from the field. Sir Henry, as governor of Worcester, vigorously held the fortress and town of Worcester against the republican army under General Fairfax. For three months, in the face of mutiny and finally hunger, the loyal governor struggled manfully, awaiting instructions from a fugitive king. When he was obliged finally to surrender, it was upon honorable terms, and the moral victory of the event abides with Sir Henry.

The fortunes of the Washington family being reversed under the rule of Cromwell, two of its members, John and Lawrence Washington, came to Virginia about the year 1657 and settled on Bridge's Creek in Westmoreland County. Here they married, established homes, and served the colony in various capacities, civil and military. It was Lawrence, the son of John, the immigrant, who became the father of the Augustine Washington who married Mary Ball. At the time of his marriage to Mary Ball, Augustine Washington was a widower, the father of two boys, Lawrence and Augustine, Jr., and a daughter, Jane.

Mary Ball is said to have been a brown-eyed beauty, toasted by the gallants of the day as "The Rose of Epping

Forest." According to Lossing, "Mr. Paulding, an early biographer, says she was described to him by those who knew her well, 'as of ordinary stature, once a great belle.' High-spirited, yet of great simplicity of manners, uncommon strength of mind and decision of character, she exacted great deference from her sons, of whom George was the favorite.

"She was inflexible in the performance of the ordinary duties of life, punctual in discharging the obligations of justice, and conscientious in the observance of those nicer social morals which, as they elude definition, are often violated without reproach."

We know from the wills of Mary Ball's father and mother that, although orphaned in childhood, she was not penniless. Her father had bequeathed her four hundred acres of land in Richmond County, "lying in ye Freshes of ye Rappahannock River" and "my negroe boy Tome and ye negroes Jo and Jack," to say nothing of the "feathers in ye kitchen loft." To these possessions her mother added "one likely young negro woman, one young mare, one good young Paceing horse," a good silk plush side saddle, two gold rings, her father's bed, "one suit of good curtains and fallens (valance), one Rugg, one Quilt, one pair Blenakets," a few pieces of table and bed linen, together with an assortment of kitchen utensils and the greater part of her wearing apparel. A half brother, John Johnson, who died soon after Mary's mother, supplemented this dowry with "all my land in Stafford county which my father-in-law Richard Hewes gave me." The husband of Mary's sister Elizabeth later bequeathed her his young dapple-gray riding horse. All in all, the young woman was left fairly well endowed. She was reared in the comfortable home of Captain (later Major) George Eskridge, described in her mother's will as "my trusty and well-beloved friend."

Scholarly accomplishments were unknown to Mary Ball, but she could always speak her mind. We may be sure that she never dallied over French verbs, but that spinning, weaving, sewing, brewing, baking, and preserving were matters of everyday practice to her. The few letters written by her are ungrammatical and misspelled, but even her illustrious son has been accused of similar deficiencies.

Augustine Washington has been described as a man of noble appearance, tall and muscular build, with brown hair, ruddy complexion, and fine gray eyes. Lossing tells us of a gun belonging to him of such size and weight that few men could aim and fire it without resting it upon some support, although he himself is said to have done so with ease.

Mary Ball, upon her marriage to Augustine Washington, became the mistress of a home not as elegant as some in Tidewater Virginia, but comfortable and ample for her needs. The government of the United States, after much research, has reconstructed this home upon the original site. It was a two-story house of red brick, containing four good-sized rooms on each floor and a brick-walled dairy in the basement, besides rooms for the use of servants in their various household activities, although they were housed in separate quarters, probably log cabins. The double chimneys at either end of the house provided warmth for each of the eight rooms, as well as the basement quarters. The fireplace of the best room was of Dutch tiles depicting scenes from the Scriptures. It was in this home, now called Wakefield, that George Washington was born.

Early biographers of the Washington family almost invariably describe Washington's birthplace as a four-roomed cottage with a lean-to at one end. Even recent writers, who have had access to authoritative material, persist in repeating this error.

The assertion that Augustine Washington and Mary Ball met in England, were married there, and there brought forth their firstborn, is probably a romantic myth. The Reverend William Meade, Bishop of Virginia, in his *Old Churches, Ministers, and Families of Virginia,** states that George Washington was born in Westmoreland County, near Pope's Creek church, and was baptized there. George Washington himself, in reply to the query of Sir Isaac Heard, in 1792, said, "I was born in Westmoreland (County), Virginia." In the light of these two pronouncements, it seems irrational to remain doubtful.

While it appears to be true that no tangible record of the Virginia marriage remains, it is probably equally true that no such English record exists or ever did exist. The point has been the subject of research, but remains a mystery, with the probabilities all pointing to the celebration of the marriage in Virginia.

However skeptical we may be as to the romantic English courtship of Augustine Washington and his second wife, we may accept the record in their family Bible of

* Published in 1857.

Augustine Washington and Mary Ball was Married the
Sixth of March, 17 30/31 :

George Washington Son to Augustine & Mary his Wife was born
y. 11th Day of February 1731/2 about 10 in the Morning & was baptized the 5th of April
following. Mr. Beverly Whiting & Capt. Christopher Brooks Godfathers and
Mrs. Mildred Gregory Godmother

Betty Washington was born the 20th of June 1733 about 6 in J. Morrow
Departed this life the 31st of March 1797 at 4 o'clock
Samuel Washington was Born y 16th Novr 1734 about 3 in y. Morrow.

14

FACSIMILE OF GEORGE WASHINGTON'S BIRTH RECORD

ington raises the ore and carts it thither for twenty shillings the ton of iron that it yields. The furnace is built on a run, which discharges its waters into the Potomac. Besides Mr. Washington and Mr. England, several other persons are concerned. Matters are very well managed, and no expense is spared to make them profitable. Mr. England can neither read nor write, but is so skilled in iron works that he has likewise the chief management of the works at Principia, at the head of the Bay, where they have erected a forge and make very good bar iron."

It was from the proceeds of his mining interests that Augustine Washington derived a good portion of his income, enabling him to send his two elder sons to England for a period of years, and later make them valuable gifts of land and other property. Had the father lived a few years longer, the circumstances of George Washington's youth would in all probability have been much different.

The facts of George's earliest years are somewhat obscured by conflicting statements, but his boyish trends are attested by his namesake and adopted son, George Washington Parke Custis, the orphaned grandson of Martha Washington. From Custis's *Memoirs of Washington* we learn that in boyhood George Washington was of rugged physique, and, although even then rather grave and reserved, was fond of sports which called for the exercise of strength and skill.

George Washington's formal education was rather unsystematically obtained, being dependent upon local schools greatly limited in their scope. We learn from the Reverend Edward Charles McGuire, who married a granddaughter of George's sister Betty, and who was for forty-five years rector of St. George's Church in Fredericksburg, that George first attended an "old-field" school* tutored by an ex-convict. He was probably a political offender brought from England by Augustine Washington, who is said to have profited by the importation of bond servants from England.

The death of Augustine Washington in his forty-ninth year undoubtedly restricted George's education. It seems quite logical to suppose that had Mr. Washington lived, he would have sent George to England to be educated, as he had sent his elder sons, Lawrence and Augustine, Jr. Dr. McGuire, in his *The Religious Opinions and Character of Washington,* makes an interesting statement as to the affection of Augustine Washington for his son George. "Between him (George) and his father it would seem that a delightful intercourse always subsisted, it being a matter of regret to the latter that he was obliged to be separated from his child even during the hours of school. Mr. Washington survived his removal from Westmoreland County but a few years. He had time enough allowed him, however, to mark the budding virtues of his son. It was in the Easter holidays that Mr. Washington was taken sick. George was absent at the time, on a visit to some of his acquaintances at Chotank. He was sent for after his father's sickness became serious, and reached the parental abode in time to witness the last struggle and receive the parting benediction of his beloved parent." Mr. McGuire wrote before the discovery

---

* Built on land exhausted by tobacco cultivation.

of the Pohick vestry book, and therefore did not know of the residence of the Washington family at Epsewasson before their removal to the farm opposite Fredericksburg. He recorded, to the best of his ability, the traditions of the family.

It is interesting to note that before his death Augustine Washington had established his two elder sons in the life of the colony, enabling them to live as gentlemen of some means. To Lawrence he had given the Epsewasson property, which he estimated at 2500 acres, with house, barn, mill, and other buildings. The gift included not only household furnishings, but horses, cattle, sheep, and hogs, as well as the negro slaves necessary to maintain the property. Lawrence, after his return from the British naval campaign in South America against the Spanish, promptly named his estate Mount Vernon, in honor of Admiral Vernon, the hero of Porto Bello.* To Augustine, Jr., commonly called Austin, Mr. Washington had given the Bridge's Creek property, completely furnished and supplied with everything necessary to a colonial gentleman of the day. This is the property now known as Wakefield. These gifts Augustine Washington confirmed in his will, a document which throws a clear light upon the economic status of the family. He bequeathed to Lawrence, as his eldest son, his interests in his iron mines in Virginia and Maryland, charging him only to buy for his brother Augustine three slaves, and to pay Betty, George's only living sister, upon her

---

* A port on the Caribbean coast of Panama, from which Spanish treasure ships sailed in the early days. It was captured by Admiral Vernon in 1740 during the war between England and Spain.

coming of age, the sum of four hundred pounds. This was a liberal wedding dowry for a young lady of the times. Betty also received two negro children by the terms of her father's will. It is a matter of some surprise that Mr. Washington's bequest to her was in favorable proportion in value to the property he bequeathed to each of her younger brothers.

To George, Mr. Washington bequeathed the Fredericksburg farm, together with ten negro slaves and a share in a piece of property on Deep Run, besides three lots in Fredericksburg.

He left in his wife's hands the administration of the property of his minor sons, George, Samuel, John Augustine, and Charles until their coming of age. In her own right Mary Ball Washington received the crops from the Bridge's Creek, Chotank, and Rappahannock "quarters," and was allowed the working of the Bridge's Creek "quarter" for five years afterwards, with the specification that within that time she might establish a "quarter" on Deep Run. These legacies left the family housed and provided for, but there were no large sums of money from which the widow might draw in educating her children.

Mary Washington took up the burden of rearing her family of four sons and their only living sister with Spartan fortitude. That she was equal to the task we have heard from all who knew her. Custis, who remembered her as she was in her declining years and had also had the benefit of acquaintance with many of her contemporaries as well as a store of traditions unstaled by time, gives us an idea of the methodical management of her home and children. He says: "The mother of Washington, in forming him for those distinguished parts he was destined to perform, first taught him the duties of obedience, the better to prepare him for those of command. In the well-ordered domicile where his early years were passed, the levity and indulgence, common to youth, were tempered by a deference and well-regulated restraint, which, while it curtailed or suppressed no rational enjoyment, usual in the springtime of life, prescribed those enjoyments within the bounds of moderation and propriety.

"The matron held in reserve an authority, which never departed from her, not even when her son had become the most illustrious of men. It seemed to say, 'I am your mother, the being who gave you life, the guide who directed your steps when they needed the guidance of age and wisdom, the parental affection which claimed your love, the parental authority which commanded your obedience; whatever may be your success, whatever your renown, next to your God you owe them to me.' Nor did the chief dissent from these truths, but to the last moments of the life of his venerable parent he yielded to her will the most dutiful and implicit obedience, and felt for her person and character the most holy reverence and attachment.

"This lady possessed not the ambition which is common to lesser minds; and the peculiar plainness, yet dignity, of her habits and manners became in no wise altered when the sun of glory rose upon her house, in the character of her child. The late Lawrence Washington Esq., of Chotank, one of associates of the juvenile years of the chief, and remembered by him in his will, thus describes the home of the mother:

" 'I was often there with George, his playmate, schoolmate, and young man's companion. Of the mother I was ten times more afraid than I ever was of my own parents. She awed me in the midst of her kindness, for she was, indeed, truly kind. I have often been present with her sons, proper tall fellows, too, and we were all as mute as mice; and even now, when time has whitened my locks, and I am the grandparent of a second generation, I could not behold that remarkable woman without feelings it is impossible to describe. Whoever has seen that awe-inspiring air and manner so characteristic in the Father of his Country, will remember the matron as she appeared when the presiding genius of her well-ordered household, commanding and being obeyed.' "

We are told that it was Mary Washington's habit to gather her children about her and read to them from the Bible or some other book selected for its moral influence. Among the books in the Washington home was Sir Matthew Hale's *Contemplations, Moral and Divine*. It bore on the fly-leaf the name of Augustine Washington's first wife, written in a clear, bold hand. Underneath the original owner's name appears the inscription, also written in a firm hand, "and Mary Washington." This book Custis remembers as being treasured

and Mary Washington

in the library of Mount Vernon and used by Washington for Sabbath reading to his family. A few extracts from the ancient volume will serve to indicate the trend of instruction which Mary Washington imparted to her children. "The greatest good that an Intellectual Creature can possibly have," writes Sir Matthew, "and that which alone is Commensurate to it, is to have itself filled with the manifestation of the Truth, Glory, Goodness, and Bounty of God. All other things are too narrow to fill the power and capacity of the Soul." Mary Washington doubtless considered this the very cornerstone of religious instruction. Can it be that she believed her growing son George to be in need of admonition: "An humble man leans not to his own understanding and trusts not in it; he is sensible of the all-sufficient Power, Wisdom, and Goodness of Almighty God, and commits himself to Him for Counsel, Guidance, Direction, and Strength." Surely the son remembered, all his life, the sweet tones of his mother's voice gravely reading this and many other passages, the truths of which sank deeply into his soul.

It became evident about this time that George was the kind of boy whom people delight in lending a helping hand over the hard places along life's pathway. Had he been their full brother, neither Lawrence nor Augustine could have shown more solicitude for his future welfare.

Augustine having married a Westmoreland heiress, George was invited to live in their home in order that he might continue his education. Here he is said to have been placed in the charge of a Mr. Williams, under whom he studied mathematics and surveying, the subjects which became the stepping-stones to widening opportunities both civil and military.

In connection with this work George began the serious study of all manner of business forms, such as notes, receipts, bills of exchange, bonds, indentures, bills of sale, land warrants, leases, deeds, and wills. Being of a very practical turn of mind, the boy carefully copied all these forms into a notebook, doubtless longing for the day to come when he might use them in actual business dealings with neighbors.

George is known to have been very fond of mathematics, and to have taken great pains in working out problems in algebra, geometry, and trigonometry. Surveying was a subject which appealed to his practical nature, and his family doubtless encouraged him in this study, as it was then quite a profitable occupation. It seems to have been something in the nature of a gentlemanly avocation as well, for his brother Lawrence was a proficient surveyor, although he made no use of the science, except, perhaps, in the management of his own property.

While the active nature of the work of surveying doubtless appealed to George, it is the beauty of his diagrams and the care and precision with which he entered every detail of his surveys that seem to be noteworthy in a lad of his age. Boundaries, angles, measurements, plots, and calculations—all are entered with formality and exactness in his books. We are told that he did not confine himself to the more simple processes of the art. Jared Sparks informs us that he used logarithms and proved the accuracy of his work by different methods.

Having exhausted the resources of Mr. Williams's school at Oak Grove, George went back to his mother's home opposite Fredericksburg. Mr. Moncure D. Conway, in his *George Washington's Rules of Civility,* sets the year as 1745, stating that an old manuscript is his authority for the fact that Lewis Willis, son of Colonel Henry Willis, was a schoolmate of George Washington. At that time the Reverend James Marye, a gentleman of French descent, was rector of St. George's church in Fredericksburg. It was very common for clergymen to supplement the religious instruction of boys with the study of the classics. Just when Mr. Marye began giving such classical training to the youths of the neighborhood is not definitely known, but there is a strong tradition that he gave George some instruction. Possibly it was under Mr. Marye that the boy began the study of Latin. On the fly-leaf of a copy of Patrick's Latin translation of Homer, printed in 1742, George wrote in the large, rough hand of his school days:

> Hunc mihi quaeso (bone Vir) Libellum
> Redde, si forsan tenues repertum.
> Ut Scias qui sum sine fraude Scriptum,
>   Est mihi nomen,
>   Georgio Washington*
>
> George Washington, Fredericksburg, Virginia

---

* This little book I pray you, good man, return to me if perchance you find it. That you may know without question who the writer is, this is my name, George Washington.

Washington never was noted as a student of Latin or any other language, but his remarkable achievements in later life have drawn attention to every detail of his early years. The famous *Rules of Civility,* which form a large part of one of his school copybooks, have received great attention. Beginning with the first, "Every Action done in Company ought to be with some Sign of Respect to those that are Present," to the last, "Labour to keep alive in your Breast that Little Spark of Celestial fire called Conscience," they are replete with moral maxims and capital letters. The tradition is that it was the Reverend Marye who presented these rules to George for his guidance. The origin of the Rules has been disputed, but the Rules remain. They cannot be dismissed from Washington's life by quibble or skepticism. That they aided him in forming the habits of perfect courtesy which distinguished him through his lifetime seems unquestionable.

This period of Washington's life is very interesting, obscure though it is. Much light has been cast on it by the letters to and from members of the Washington family published in Moncure D. Conway's *Barons of the Potomac and the Rappahannock.* These letters have been pronounced genuine.

It is Custis who records the fact that such was young George's confidence in his own strength that he attempted to tame an unmanageable colt, with the result that the animal fell dead under him, having burst a blood vessel in the struggle to unseat his rider. It was on the occasion of George's confession of his responsibility for this misfortune that Mary Washington compressed her lips to refrain from giving utterance to the anger that flashed in her eyes. After a momentary struggle with her feelings, she said calmly: "While I regret the loss of my favorite, I rejoice in my son, who always speaks the truth."

It was at this time that George cast longing eyes upon the ships which sailed up and down the Rappahannock. Perhaps partly influenced by his father's seafaring enterprises, George dreamed of a life at sea. He was then, at the age of fifteen, as tall as most men, with great strength and endurance. Furthermore, he felt himself able to do what any man could do, and he longed to make a career for himself in the world of men. With the restlessness of youth, his thoughts turned from the placid life of a farmer to the adventurous roving of a sailor.

His mother did not sympathize with this ambition of his, and such was her love for him that she could not bear the thought of parting from him. In her anxiety she wrote to her brother, Joseph Ball, who had spent some time in Virginia, but lived in England, where he practiced law. Joseph Ball's letter, coupled with Mrs. Washington's desire to keep her son at home, put a stop to George's dreams of a seafaring life. A glimpse of that letter, which may have been of great consequence in determining the fate of nations, may prove interesting. It is dated Stratford-by-Bow, 19th May, 1747, and reads:

"I understand that you are advised and have some thoughts of putting your son George to sea. I think he had better be put apprentice to a tinker, for a common sailor before the mast has by no means the common liberty of the subject; for they will press him from a ship where he has fifty shillings a month and make him take twenty-three, and cut, and slash, and use him like a negro, or rather like a dog. And, as to any considerable preferment in the navy, it is not to be expected, as there are always so many gaping for it here who have interest, and he has none. And if he should get to be master of a Virginia ship (which is very difficult to do), a planter that has three or four hundred acres of land and three or four slaves, if he be industrious, may live more comfortably, and leave his family in better bread, than such a master of a ship can . . . He must not be too hasty to be rich, but go on gently and with patience, as things will naturally go. This method, without aiming at being a fine gentleman before his time, will carry a man more comfortably and surely through the world than going to sea, unless it be a great chance indeed. I pray God keep you and yours. Your loving brother,

"Joseph Ball."

His mother's tears, reinforced by the cold, hard judgment of his Uncle Joseph, put an end to George's dream of riches and glory to be wrested from the sea.

We perceive from outstanding events of his life that in later years emotion frequently conflicted with judgment, but was always so controlled by consideration of justice as to carry no weight in the ultimate decision.

CHAPTER II

IN THE WILDERNESS

Prevented from realizing his cherished dream of going to sea, George was at a loss as to what to do next. In his dilemma, he turned to his brother, Lawrence, for counsel.

Lawrence was happily settled at Mount Vernon, having married Anne, the daughter of Colonel Fairfax, of Belvoir, a neighboring estate. Colonel Fairfax was the American agent of his cousin, Thomas, Lord Fairfax, who owned a tract of land so immense that its western boundaries had not even been defined. Squatters were settling upon some of the choicest parts of it, and even the Crown, in ignorance of the true boundaries, was granting parts of the land to others. Land-lover that he was, Lord Fairfax came to Virginia to define his boundaries and to take formal possession.

George, having demonstrated his ability as a surveyor by making skillfully-drawn plats of Mount Vernon's pastures and turnip fields, was now engaged in a subordinate capacity in the survey of Lord Fairfax's wilderness land. A licensed, official surveyor, Mr. James Genn, was in charge of the work, and a number of young men were members of the party in various capacities. Young George Washington was one of the number and not the leader of the expedition, as is frequently stated, although it is true that he was the friend and intimate of George

William Fairfax, whose sister Anne had married Lawrence Washington. George William Fairfax had been
educated in England, and, upon his return to Virginia,
was given the management of Lord Fairfax's western
lands, succeeding in that office his father, the colonel,
who wished to give more time to his eastern affairs.

The life of a surveyor of the wilderness was a hardy
one. In the surveying of the Fairfax tract of nearly six
million acres young Washington became inured to long
travels, afoot or on horseback; to hunting his meat and
cooking it over a campfire; and to sleeping in a tent or
under the open stars. It was during this expedition that
he had his first glimpse of Indians in their wild state,
as well as his first contact with white people whose language he could not understand and whom he designated
as "Dutch." In the midst of new scenes and new impressions crowded into each day, young George performed his work with such exactness that no flaw has
yet been found therein. It was this accuracy which led
to his being granted a license as official surveyor of Cul-
pepper County in the following year.

After embarking upon his career as official surveyor,
George's work took him here, there, and everywhere.
Sometimes he was with his mother at Fredericksburg;
sometimes at Mount Vernon with Lawrence; sometimes
at Bridge's Creek with Augustine. He also spent some
time at Greenway Court, the rustic home which Lord
Fairfax had built in the heart of his wilderness land, and
while there had access to his lordship's library, a fine
one for the times. George's diary, at this period, records
his reading *The Spectator* and also a considerable amount
of English history.

Lossing's estimate of young Washington's personality and activities during his surveying years appears to be a true one.

"His experience as a surveyor was eminently favorable to the development of his strength and activity of muscle and limb. From childhood his frame had seemed precociously large and vigorous, and now he had reached a maturity of physical energy, a firmness, size, and symmetry of person, and a hardihood of temperament, such as men of his inherited social position have rarely been able to acquire.

"He thoroughly acquainted himself with the habits and feelings of the frontier settlers, the outer and expanding circle of civilization, who at this time constituted a large proportion of the whole population of the country. Their log cabins, scattered at remote distances through the forest, afforded him shelter from night or storm, and in his familiar intercourse with them, around the hearth or in the fields, he learned their character and the influences by which they were most apt to be moved; and he himself also became extensively known to these backwoodsmen, and the simplicity, frankness, and earnestness of his nature must have made the most favorable impressions; so that when an army was to be made up largely of individuals of this description, and deriving from them its chief moral and physical qualities, he was found above all men fitted to appreciate its efficiency and command its confidence.

"In these years he had also ample opportunities for studying the character and temper of the Indians, whose predatory or vengeful incursions upon the settlements had at one time or another brought mourning into almost every household, and whose uncertain dispositions made them a continual terror not only to women and children but to the most bold-spirited and sagacious invaders of the forests. He saw them stealthily following the wild game on the mountains, and in their wigwam, about their council fires, or celebrating their prowess in fraternal wars; and was so careful and wise an observer of their peculiarities that during his subsequent military and civil administrations few were as good judges as to the best modes of dealing with them.

"There are not many things more important or essential to a great commander than a proper education of the eye. The quick glance which accurately measures distances, numbers, or elevations, as it ranges across the battlefield through clouds of smoke and bristling rows of bayonets, is in most cases a result of long experience in the conduct, arrangement, and disposition of armies. Washington's observation as a surveyor enabled him to estimate with astounding rapidity and certainty the features and capacities of fields as large as his vision comprehended, so that he could direct the movements of forces in such a manner as to be assured of every advantage within his reach that depended on the favorable accidents of nature.

"On the whole, it would be difficult to conceive of any manner in which Washington might have passed this portion of his life more advantageously, either with reference to his private interest or his preparation for the great work before him."

Although so exact and painstaking in his work as

Washington

surveyor, George felt that the profession did not provide sufficient outlet for his boundless energies and aspirations. Whenever an idle interval found him at Mount Vernon, he took up the study of the military profession. Two of Lawrence's former comrades-in-arms proved helpful in this respect. These were Jacob Van Braam, who instructed the youth in the art of fencing, and Adjutant Muse, who drilled him in military exercises, evolutions in the field, and military tactics in general. At this period of his life George's tongue was likely to fail him when he most wanted words, but when Lawrence and his military friends reviewed their experiences in the French and Spanish wars, George was an eager listener.

About this time it became evident that Virginia was likely to be plunged into the war between the English and the French. The colony was therefore divided into four districts. An officer, called an adjutant general, was appointed for each district. He was given the rank of major and a salary of one hundred fifty pounds a year, his duty being to assemble and exercise the militia, inspect their arms and equipment, and enforce discipline. Probably through the influence of Lawrence and the Fairfaxes, George was appointed for his district.

His military career had hardly begun when the state of Lawrence's health became alarming. The privations incident upon the South American campaign had undermined his health, and consumption had set in. He was advised to try the air of the West Indies, and in September, 1751, he sailed for Barbados, accompanied by George. This was the first and only journey outside of his native land that George Washington ever embarked upon, although he was to traverse the thirteen colonies in later years. Poor Lawrence had only a temporary relief from his malady and came back to Virginia within a year to die under his own roof. George, although the youngest of Lawrence's executors, was so familiar with his affairs that the business of settling the estate was left in his hands. This is another instance of the confidence universally placed in the judgment of the tall, reserved young man of nineteen.*

It is evident that at this age, when many young men appear to be but thoughtless striplings, Washington was possessed of that impressiveness of personality which characterized his later years. Even then he had a peculiar facility for doing the one thing incontestably right under any circumstance. His proclivities were all of a nature calling for strenuous endeavor. So it is not surprising that he much preferred the stirring life of camp and forest to dalliance in drawing-rooms, where he was generally silent and awkward.

At this time French activities in territory claimed by the British necessitated expostulation. Governor Dinwiddie looked about for someone to undertake this deli-

* Some years later Washington came into possession of Mount Vernon.

cate mission. What man could be depended upon to make his way through hundreds of miles of wilderness, through the lands of hostile Indians, to the French outposts, there to deliver a letter to the commandant?

It was near the end of October, and the journey would be one of great hardship. Several men were approached, but no one wanted to go. Then Major Washington was approached and accepted. He had spent years surveying wilderness lands, and the forest held no terrors for him.

Accordingly, Governor Dinwiddie gave him a commission and instruction to perform the hazardous mission. The young major left Williamsburg, Virginia, accompanied by a party of men, among whom were Van Braam, who understood French as imperfectly as he did English, and a John Davidson, who imperfectly understood the Indian tongues. On the way to the French outposts Washington was to visit friendly Indian chiefs for the purpose of strengthening their allegiance, and he was to make inquiries as to the plans of the French, their numbers, and military strength. The difficult trip was accomplished successfully; so also was young Washington's first attempt at diplomacy, with the French commandant.

On the way back to Williamsburg the party had its first encounter with unfriendly Indians. In his own words Washington tells about it: "We fell in with a party of French Indians, who had lain in wait for us. One of them fired at Mr. Gist or me, not fifteen steps off, but fortunately missed. We took the fellow into custody, and kept him till nine o'clock, and then let him go, and walked all the remaining part of the night, without making any stop, that we might get the start so far as to be out of the reach of their pursuit the next day, since we were well assured they would follow our track as soon as it was light."

The Indians were not again seen or heard of, however, and soon after sunset the next evening the travelers came to the Allegheny River, where they thought themselves "safe enough to sleep." They had hoped to be able to cross over on the ice; but they were disappointed, as the river had frozen only a few yards on each side, and great quantities of ice were driving down the current.

Travel-worn, and exhausted with privation, cold, and excitement, they were compelled to wrap themselves in their blankets and lie down in the snow; and when morning came, the prospect of being able to cross the river seemed almost desperate. "There was no way of getting over," Washington writes, "but on a raft, which we set about with but one poor hatchet, and finished just after sunset. This was a whole day's work. We next got it launched, and went on board of it; then set off; but before we were half way over, we were jammed in the ice in such a manner that we expected every moment our raft would sink and ourselves perish. I put out my setting pole to try and stop the raft, that the ice might pass by, when the rapidity of the stream threw it with so much violence against the pole that it jerked me over, into ten feet of water; but I fortunately saved myself by catching hold of one of the raft logs. Notwithstanding all our efforts, we could not get the raft to either shore, but were obliged, as we were near an island, to quit our raft and make to it."

They reached the island at dusk and spent a miserable night without the means of making a fire and with their clothes freezing upon them. By morning Mr. Gist's hands and feet were frozen, but the very severity of the weather saved their lives. The ice being strong enough to bear their weight, they crossed safely. Before another nightfall they arrived at Mr. Frazier's trading post, where they were made welcome. There they had to remain two or three days before they could resume their journey.

The report of this mission was published by order of the governor. It was widely copied in colonial newspapers, and reprinted in London by official order, thus making Washington a figure of international note at the age of twenty-one.

It was during the campaign to repel the French from the Ohio country that Washington protested against the economy which allowed colonial officers a smaller compensation than that received by those of the regular army. That this feeling was general among the colonials is indicated by Washington's letter to the governor:

"Nothing prevents them from throwing down their commissions but the approaching danger, which has too far engaged their honor for them to recede till other officers are sent in their room, or an alteration is made in their pay, during which time they will assist with their best endeavors voluntarily; that is, without receiving the gratuity allowed by the resolves of the committee.

"I have a constitution hardy enough to encounter and undergo the most severe trials, and, I flatter myself, resolution to face what any man dares; and I will with the greatest pleasure devote my services to the expedition, without any other reward than the satisfaction of serving my country; but to be slaving dangerously for only the shadow of pay, through the woods, rocks, mountains —I would rather dig for a maintenance, provided I were reduced to the necessity, than serve upon such ignoble terms; for I really do not see why the lives of his majesty's subjects in Virginia should be of less value than those of his subjects in other parts of his American dominions, especially when it is well known that we must undergo double their hardships." Lossing states that although it was the indignity involved in the proposition of the government that induced this manifestation of feeling, he took care to set before the governor the absolute injustice of the pay which was offered. " 'Now,' wrote Washington, 'if we could be fortunate enough to drive the French from the Ohio, as far as your honor would please to have them sent, in any short time, our pay will not be sufficient to discharge our first expenses. I would not have you imagine from this that I have said all these things to have our pay increased, but to justify myself, and to show you that our complaints are not frivolous, but founded in strict reason.

" 'The motives which have led me here are pure and noble; I had no view of acquisition, but that of honor, by serving my king and country.

" 'Be the consequences what they will, I am determined not to leave the regiment, but to be among the last men to quit the Ohio, even if I serve as a private volunteer, which I greatly prefer to the establishment we are now upon.' "

There is much interesting correspondence concerning the conduct of the campaign, and one letter to Dinwiddie reveals something of the tenacity for which Washington was later distinguished.

"I shall expect every hour to be attacked, and by unequal numbers, which I must withstand, if there are five to one, for I fear the consequence will be that we shall lose the Indians if we suffer ourselves to be driven back —and I will not be surprised, let them come at what hour they will, and this is as much as I can promise; but my best endeavors shall not be wanting to effect more. I doubt not, if you hear I am beaten, you will hear at the same time that we have done our duty in fighting as long as there is a shadow of hope."

It was in the course of this campaign that, owing to the death of his superior officer, Colonel Joshua Fry, Washington was elevated to the command of the expedition. This proved an embarrassing honor, for he found that British officers of the regular army refused to be commanded by colonial officers, apparently regarding them in much the same light that they did the Indians.

Upon receiving a message from Tanacharisson, a friendly Indian chief, warning him against an attack from the French, Washington prepared for the worst. An encounter ensued, in which the French lost ten men, among them Monsieur de Jumonville, the commander of the small force engaged. Soon afterwards Jumonville's brother set out from Fort Duquesne with five hundred men. They attacked Washington's three hundred men at Great Meadows, where Washington had fortified himself behind a rough stockade, which he had named "Fort

Necessity." The French were victorious in this encounter, and Washington was obliged to surrender, though he insisted upon honorable terms.

In the articles of surrender the death of Jumonville was named *assassination,* which escaped Washington at the time, but confounded him later. The terms of surrender are said to have been interpreted to him by the light of a candle frequently put out by wind and rain, but when the terms were published, they were read in the clear light of day.

Washington did not learn the true meaning of the word until after their publication by M. De Villiers. Writing to a friend, he said, "If the gentleman (De Villiers) in his account had adhered to the truth, he must have confessed that we looked upon the offer to parley as an artifice to get into and examine our trenches, and refused, on this account, until they desired an officer might be sent to them, and gave their parole for his safe return. He might also, if he had been as great a lover of the truth as he was of vainglory, have said that we absolutely refused their first and second proposals, and would consent to capitulate on no other terms than such as we obtained. That we were willfully or ignorantly deceived by our interpreter in regard to the word *assassination,* I do aver, and will to my dying moment; so will every officer that was present. The interpreter was a Dutchman, little acquainted with the English tongue, and therefore might not advert to the tone and meaning of the word in English; but, whatever his motives were for so doing, certain it is he called it the *death,* or the *loss,* of the Sieur Jumonville. So we received and so we understood it, until, to our great surprise and mortification, we found it otherwise in a literal translation.

"That we left our baggage and horses at the Meadows is certain; that there was not even a possibility to bring them away is equally certain, as we had every horse belonging to the camp killed or taken away during the action; so that it was impracticable to bring anything off that our shoulders were not able to bear; and to wait there was impossible, for we had scarce three days' provisions, and were seventy miles from a supply; yet, to say we came off precipitately is absolutely false; notwithstanding they did, contrary to articles, suffer their Indians to pillage our baggage, and commit all kinds of irregularity, we were with them until ten o'clock the next day; we destroyed our powder and other stores, nay, even our private baggage, to prevent its falling into their hands, as we could not bring it off. When we had got about a mile from the place of action, we missed two or three of the wounded, and sent a party back to bring them up; this is the party he speaks of. We brought them all safe off, and encamped within three miles of the Meadows. These are circumstances, I think, that make it evidently clear that we were not very apprehensive of danger."

The crowning recognition of his best endeavors under conditions of great hardship, however, was his reduction from the rank of colonel to that of captain. Innate pride made it impossible for Washington to accept this degradation. Indignantly he resigned his commission and retired to private life.

When General Braddock at length arrived in America with an elaborate plan for driving the French from their outposts, he may have felt the desirability of consultation with one who had participated in the preceding skirmishes. He overcame young Washington's scruples by inviting him to be a member of his staff as aid-de-camp. It was the opportunity to increase his knowledge of the military profession that enticed Washington from his home. His own words follow: "My friends may conceive that some advantageous offers have engaged my services, when, in reality, it is otherwise, for I expect to be a considerable loser in my private affairs by going. It is true, I have been importuned to make the campaign by General Braddock, as a member of his family, he conceiving, I suppose, that the small knowledge I have had an opportunity of acquiring, of the country and the Indians, is worthy of his notice, and may be useful to him in the progress of the expedition."

This decision, however welcome to his friends, alarmed his mother. She journeyed from Fredericksburg to Mount Vernon in a vain attempt to keep her son at home in safety. On this occasion, being unfortified by the advice of her brother Joseph, she was obliged to let her enterprising son have his own way.

But if George, at the age of twenty-three, was possessed of a tenacity amounting almost to obstinacy, he met his match in Braddock. That general, on being advised of the dangers of Indian ambuscades, smiled as he replied, "These savages may indeed be a formidable enemy to raw American militia, but upon the king's regular and disciplined troops, sir, it is impossible they should make an impression."

Braddock, the "soldier of the schools," gazed with surprised disdain upon Captain Jack, a well-known frontiersman, whom the Indians of western Pennsylvania dreaded more than any other enemy. Captain Jack appeared before Braddock in forest attire of fringed hunting shirt, leggings, and moccasins, armed with a straight-shooting rifle and a well-sharpened hunting-knife. He offered the services of himself and a party of frontiersmen as scouts, to serve as a reconnoitering party to forestall Indian ambuscades. This was a contingency with which Braddock was entirely unacquainted, but he replied that he had experienced troops on whom he could depend for all purposes. The Indian fighters were highly offended and retired to the forests.

Braddock, who loved a military show, could not forego marching his redcoats through the woods in regular columns, announcing their progress with the music of fife and drum. Washington is said to have advised against such bold procedure. There has been some dispute as to whether the French or the British opened the engagement. It appears that the French met the British with a defense so fierce and effective that the result surprised themselves as much as it did the English.

Braddock's men, penned in the narrow road which they were cutting through the woods, were as unable to defend themselves as they were to make an effectual attack. The carefully-drilled British brought their artillery into play, but could see nothing to aim at but trees and shrubbery. Braddock did his best to extricate his forces from the slaughter which followed. Washington, weakened by illness, rode from place to place along the line, through the thickest of the fighting, trying to bring up reinforcements. Two horses were killed under him, and four bullets passed through his coat. Miraculously, he was the only mounted officer who escaped injury.

Too late Braddock realized the folly of allowing his troops to be caught in a place from which they could neither advance nor retreat with safety, but were cut down by the "shoot and hide" methods of the Indians. And he finally ordered the retreat which his regulars had anticipated, though not in platoon formation. Fighting to the last, the English general was carried mortally wounded from the field. Surviving British and American officers withdrew their men as best they could.

Washington later relieved his feelings in a letter to Dinwiddie: "The Virginia companies," he wrote, "behaved like men, and died like soldiers; for, I believe, of three companies on the ground, scarce thirty men were left alive. Captain Peyroney and all his officers, down to a corporal, were killed. Captain Polson had almost as hard a fate, for only one of his escaped. In short, the dastardly conduct of the regular troops, so called, exposed those who were inclined to do their duty to almost certain death; and, at length, in spite of every effort to the contrary, they broke, and ran as sheep before hounds, leaving the artillery, ammunition, baggage, provisions, and, in short, everything, a prey to the enemy; and when we endeavored to rally them, in hopes of regaining the ground and what we had left upon it, it was with as little success as if we had attempted to stop the wild bears of the mountains."

Washington, unable to shake off his illness, retired to

Mount Vernon to recuperate and to reflect, in a letter to his brother Augustine: "I was employed to go a journey, in the winter, when I believe few or none would have undertaken it; and what did I get by it? My expenses borne! I was then appointed, with trifling pay, to conduct a handful of men to the Ohio. What did I get by that? Why, after putting myself to a considerable expense in equipping and providing necessaries for the campaign, I went out, was soundly beaten, and lost all! Came in, and had my commission taken from me; or, in other words, my command reduced, under pretense of an order from home. I next went out a volunteer, with General Braddock, and lost all my horses, and many other things. But this, being a voluntary act, I ought not to have mentioned it; nor should I have done so, were it not to show that I have been on the losing side ever since I entered the service, which is now nearly two years."

His mother, whose loving solicitude for him never ceased, tried to dissuade him from further participation in frontier warfare. His reply, August 15, 1755, gives a hint of his desire to be more engrossingly occupied than in the management of his private affairs. "If it is in my power to avoid going to the Ohio again, I shall; but if the command is pressed upon me by the general voice of the country, and offered upon such terms as cannot be objected against, it would reflect dishonor on me to refuse it; and that, I am sure, must, and ought, to give you greater uneasiness than my going in an honorable command. Upon no other terms will I accept it. At present I have no proposals made to me, nor have I any advice of such an intention, except from private hands."

Lossing tells us that in another letter of the same date to Mr. Warner Lewis, at Williamsburg, "he expressed the belief that the command of the army could not be obtained for him upon terms that he would accept. The most important conditions which he mentioned were that he should be allowed to choose his own officers, and that there should be a better system of military regulations, more promptness in paying the troops, and a thorough reform in all the agencies for procuring supplies.

"Before these letters were written, however, Washington had been appointed commander of all the forces raised or to be raised in Virginia, upon the very conditions he had thus announced to his friend, and with the privilege of choosing an aid-de-camp and secretary."

The Assembly voted awards to all Virginians "for their gallant behavior and losses" in the battle near Duquesne, Washington's reward being three hundred pounds, the largest sum awarded.

It was impossible now for energetic Washington to remain quietly upon his farm. In the following year the Assembly authorized the erection of a chain of forts to extend from the Potomac to the North Carolina line, through the Allegheny Mountains. Washington disapproved the project but, his health restored, did all in his power to make the forts effective. It was inevitable that he should be singled out by jealousy for every insinuation of neglect and inefficiency possible. Governor Dinwiddie himself appears to have been willing to harass and hamper the young commander with perplexing interferences and ambiguous orders. Washington complained of this in letters to his friend John Robinson, the Speaker of the Assembly, saying in one, "The orders I receive are full of ambiguity. I am left, like a wanderer in the wilderness, to proceed at hazard. I am answerable for consequences, and blamed, without the privilege of defense." In another he said: "My orders are dark, doubtful, and uncertain; today approved, tomorrow condemned. . . However, I am determined to bear up under all these embarrassments some time longer, in hope of a better regulation on the arrival of Lord Loudoun, to whom I look for the future fate of Virginia."

To his kinsman in London, Richard Washington, he wrote in April, 1757: "I have been posted, then, for twenty months past, upon our cold and barren frontiers, to perform, I think, I may say, impossibilities; that is, to protect from the cruel incursions of a crafty, savage enemy a line of inhabitants more than three hundred and fifty miles in extent, with a force inadequate to the task. By this means I am become, in a manner, an exile."

All the while the Indians were raiding exposed settlements with the murderous brutality which characterized their warfare. Their depredations could hardly be called warfare, for they frequently attacked defenseless homes, setting fire to the buildings and killing the women and children in the absence of the men. These atrocities drew from Washington many expressions of anguish and concern. In October, 1757, he wrote to Speaker Robinson: "I do not know on whom these miserable, undone people are to rely for protection. If the Assembly are to give it to them, it is time that measures were at least concerting, and not when they ought to be going into execution, as has always been the case. If they are to seek it from their commander-in-chief, it is time their condition was made known to him; for I cannot forbear repeating again, that while we pursue defensive measures we pursue inevitable ruin, the loss of the country being the inevitable and fatal consequence."

To Colonel Stanwix he wrote: "I exert every means in my power to protect a much-distressed country, but it is a task too arduous. To think of defending a frontier of more than three hundred and fifty miles' extent, with only seven hundred men, is vain and idle, especially when that frontier lies more contiguous to the enemy than any other. I am, and have for a long time been, fully convinced that if we continue to pursue a defensive plan, the country must inevitably be lost."

These letters were unproductive of results except as they may have eased the young commander's mind. His health at length suffered from the rigors of frontier life, and in November he was obliged to return home. Arriving at Mount Vernon, he was prostrated by a fever which continued for months.

In February, 1758, he wrote to Colonel Stanwix: "I have never been able to return to my command since I wrote to you last, my disorder at times returning obstinately upon me, in spite of the efforts of all the sons of Aesculapius whom I have hitherto consulted. At certain periods I have been reduced to great extremity, and have now too much reason to apprehend an approaching decay, being visited with several symptoms of such a disease. I am at this time under a strict regimen, and shall set out tomorrow for Williamsburg, to receive the advice of the best physicians there. My constitution is much impaired, and nothing can retrieve it but the greatest care and the most circumspect course of life. This being the case, as I have now no prospect left or preferment in the military way, and despair of rendering that immediate service which my country may require from the person commanding its troops, I have thought of quitting my command, and retiring from all public business, leaving my post to be filled by some other person more capable of the task, and who may, perhaps, have his endeavors crowned with better success than mine have been."

Contrary to his expectations, however, Colonel Washington's health improved. It was at an opportune time, for the Assembly had acted upon Minister Pitt's recommendation to proceed against Fort Duquesne. It increased the forces of the colony to two thousand men, besides making other provisions. The troops were formed into two regiments, the one under Colonel Washington; the other under Colonel Byrd, of Westover.

Washington began at once to get his troops in readiness for the expedition against Fort Duquesne. He was obliged to make constant demands for the simplest necessities for his troops. In July, 1758, he wrote Colonel Boquet, informing him of his arrival at Fort Cumberland, and adding: "My men are very bare of regimental clothing, and I have no prospect of a supply." He surprised the good Boquet by advocating an innovation in military accouterment, saying: "So far from regretting this want during the present campaign, if I were left to pursue my own inclination, I would not only order the men to adopt the Indian dress, but cause the officers to do it also, and be the first to set the example myself. Nothing but the uncertainty of obtaining the general approbation causes me to hesitate a moment to leave my regimentals at this place, and proceed as light as any Indian in the woods. It is an unbecoming dress, I own, for an officer; but convenience, rather than show, should be consulted."

Boquet received the suggestion enthusiastically, and the experiment was tried. Washington equipped two companies in this way, and sent them to headquarters. The weather was extremely hot, and the wearers of the novel costume were well pleased. It was not to be expected, however, that British regular troops should discard their brilliant uniforms, however uncomfortable, merely at the suggestion of a provincial colonel. Their blind adherence to tradition forbade, although some of them lived to see themselves opposed by American riflemen thus attired.

After a great deal of bickering as to the best route, and still more exertion in making their way through the wilderness, the British approached Fort Duquesne in high spirits, although encountering in the forest the bones of those who had perished under Braddock. Great was Washington's joy when he was able to write to Governor Fauquier: "The enemy, after letting us get within a day's march of the place, burned the fort, and ran away by the light of it, at night, going down the Ohio by water, to the number of about five hundred, according to our best information."

After the first jubilant raising of the British flag over the smoking ruins of the fort, the whole army, officers and men, set about burying the remains of those slain under Braddock.

The fort was rebuilt, and with joyful ceremony renamed Fort Pitt, in honor of the liberal minister who had been largely responsible for making provision for the campaign. The Indians, believing that the Great Spirit had deserted the French, submitted to those in power, and ceased their depredations upon English settlers.

Washington retired from Fort Pitt, though not without leaving a part of his forces there. On behalf of this garrison he wrote to Governor Fauquier, urging that they be supplied with clothing. With winter coming on, he made no more recommendations for the Indian style of clothing, but said plainly: "Our men are in such a miserable condition, having hardly rags to cover their nakedness, and exposed to the inclemency of the weather in this rigorous season, that, unless provision is made by the country for supplying them immediately, they must perish."

For five years Washington had labored to the point of exhaustion, in the face of all the difficulties which a mean-spirited governor, later proved dishonest, could put in his way. The peace of the frontier now appearing assured, he resigned his commission and retired to private life.

CHAPTER III

MOUNT VERNON

Although an admirer of fair ladies from his early youth, Washington remained a bachelor until he reached the age of twenty-seven. We know that in his teens he sighed for a "Lowland Beauty," whose identity remains a mystery to this day. She may have been pretty Betsy Fauntleroy, to whose grandfather, in the year 1752, Washington addressed a letter "hoping for a revocation of the former cruel sentence." We are told that the beautiful Betsy was much sought after, and it may be that she thought the bashful young surveyor, whose military career was then only dawning, a poor choice. No doubt she had other suitors who were more graceful in the drawing-room, and who could turn a prettier phrase in love-making than the overgrown young man whose prospects did not seem outstandingly promising. At any rate, her second sentence must have been as cruel as her first, for the Fauntleroy correspondence ended where it began.

The next onslaught upon Washington's affections was innocently and unwittingly made by Miss Mary Phillipse, an heiress, also much sought after. It occurred during Washington's New England trip, in the year 1756, made for the purpose of seeking redress by appeal to General Shirley, commander-in-chief of the British forces in America, from certain troublesome questions of ranking which caused friction between British officers of the regular army and those of the colonial forces. This trip of five hundred miles, from the Virginia frontier to Boston, made entirely on horseback in the dead of winter, is another illustration of the physical stamina of the young colonel as well as of his enterprise in the attainment of his military convictions.

In the pursuit of more personal happiness, however, he was less self-assured. On his way to Boston, while in New York, he was entertained by Mr. Beverly Robinson, son of the Speaker, to whom, in an ever-flowing stream of ink, he poured out his military difficulties during the entire period of his French and Indian activities. Mr. Robinson had married a member of the wealthy and powerful Phillipse family, and it was to their hospitable manor in New York that the young colonel was invited. He was there introduced to Mrs. Robinson's sister, the attractive Miss Mary. So formidable did the loveliness of Miss Mary appear to the young man fresh from the frontier that he departed without making his admiration known to her.

At the headquarters of General Shirley, in Boston, Washington's courage revived, and he stated his difficulties with such dignity as to secure the redress he desired. We are told that General Shirley received him very politely and that he was the object of much notice because of his bravery under Braddock and his miraculous escape from the slaughter of that day.

On his way back to Virginia, Washington stopped again at the Robinson home. But the intrepid officer, who had so effectively pleaded his cause before the highest military tribunal of the land, found himself unable to express his feelings to the young woman. The warrior who had braved the fury of the savage, trembled before a pair of bright eyes. As silently as he had come, he rode back to the wilderness to give voice to his disgust for the ineffective manner in which Governor Dinwiddie directed the protection of the settlers.

In the spring of the year before his retirement, Washington had gone to Williamsburg to lay before the Assembly the needs of his men for the coming campaign. With his usual impetuosity, he had been riding hard to make all speed, when he was halted by an unforeseen circumstance. Let Custis, the grandson of Martha Washington, relate the incident in his quaint style:

"It was in 1758 that an officer, attired in a military undress, and attended by a body-servant, tall and *militaire* as his chief, crossed the ferry called William's, over the Pamunkey, a branch of the York River. On the boat touching the southern, or New Kent, side the soldier's progress was arrested by one of those personages who give the beau ideal of the Virginia gentleman of the old régime, the very soul of kindliness and hospitality. It was in vain the soldier urged his business at Williamsburg, important communications to the governor, etc. Mr. Chamberlayne, on whose domain the *militaire* had just landed, would hear of no excuse. Colonel Washington (for the soldier was he) was a name and character so dear to all the Virginians that his passing by one of the old castles of the commonwealth, without calling and partaking of the hospitalities of the host, was entirely out of the question. The colonel, however, did not surrender at discretion, but stoutly maintained his ground, till Chamberlayne, bringing up his reserve, in the intimation that he would introduce his friend to a young and charming widow, then beneath his roof, the soldier capitulated, on condition that he should dine, 'only dine,' and then, by pressing his charger and borrowing of the night, he would reach Williamsburg before his Excellency could shake off his morning slumbers. Orders were accordingly issued to Bishop, the colonel's body-servant and faithful follower, who, together with the fine English charger, had been bequeathed by the dying Braddock to Major Washington, on the famed and fatal field of the Monongahela.

"The Colonel now proceeded to the mansion, and was introduced to various guests (for when was a Virginia domicile of the olden time without guests?), and above all, to the charming widow. Tradition relates that they were mutually pleased on their first interview; nor is it remarkable. For they were of an age when impressions are strongest. The lady was fair to behold, of fascinating manners, and splendidly endowed with worldly benefits. The hero, fresh from his early fields, redolent of fame, and with a form on which 'every god did seem to set his seal, to give the world assurance of a man.'

"The morning passed pleasantly away. Evening came, with Bishop true to his orders and firm at his post. The sun sank in the horizon, and yet the colonel appeared not. And then the old soldier marveled at his chief's delay. Surely he was not wont to be a single moment behind his appointments, for he was the most punctual of all men. Meantime, the host enjoyed the scene of the veteran on duty at the gate, while the colonel was so agreeably employed in the parlor. And proclaiming that no guest ever left his house after sunset, his military visitor was without much difficulty persuaded to order Bishop to put up the horses for the night. The sun rode high in the heavens the ensuing day, when the enamored soldier pressed with his spur the charger's side, and speeded on his way to the seat of government, where, having dispatched his public business, he retraced his steps, and, at the White House (the home of Mrs. Custis) the engagement took place, with preparations for the marriage."

George Washington was married to Mrs. Martha Custis on January sixth, 1759. Both bride and groom were of aristocratic lineage, and the social prominence of the bride no less than the military renown of the groom made the occasion one long to be remembered by all who participated in it.

At the time of her marriage to Colonel Washington Mrs. Custis had two children by her previous marriage, John Parke Custis and Martha Parke Custis. From the pen of the son of John Custis, many years later, we get the following recollections of an old retainer:

"And so you remember when Colonel Washington came a-courting of your mistress?" said the biographer to old Cully, in his hundredth year. "Ay, master, that I do," replied this ancient family servant, who had lived to see five generations; "great times, sir, great times! Shall never see the like again!"—"And Washington looked something like a man, a proper man; hey, Cully?"—"Never see'd the like, sir; never the like of him, though I have seen many in my day; so tall, so straight! and then he sat a horse and rode with such an air! Ah, sir, he was like no one else! Many of the grandest gentlemen, in their gold lace, were at the wedding, but none looked like the man himself!"

"The man himself" must indeed have appeared quite handsome, dressed, as he was, in blue cloth, trimmed with silver lace, especially since his coat is said to have been lined with red silk. An embroidered white satin waistcoat added to his glory, as did a small dress-sword and gold knee- and shoe-buckles.

The bride was resplendent in a white satin gown with quilted petticoat, and overskirt of heavy, corded white silk, the silk being interwoven with threads of silver. The low, square neck of her bodice was edged with point lace, which also appeared on the puffed elbow sleeves. Her slippers were of white satin, with diamond buckles. Strings of pearls ornamented her powdered hair, and pearls gleamed in her ears and on her neck and wrist.

Colonel Washington did not at once take his bride to Mount Vernon. During the previous year Washington had been elected to the House of Burgesses in Virginia. The meetings of that body being held at Williamsburg, near the home of the bride, the young couple remained there for several months following their wedding. When the House of Burgesses met, in January, it resolved to extend a vote of thanks to Washington for his services to this country. His good friend John Robinson was Speaker of the House, and to him fell the task of extending this formal recognition.

The dignified Speaker, a master of oratory and eloquence, tendered the compliment with all the arts at his command. In resounding periods he gave utterance to a panegyric of such impressive fervency as to dumfound the heroic subject thereof. In the hush of expectancy which followed the Speaker's oration Colonel Washington rose to reply, but such was his confusion and discomfiture that he was unable to utter a word. Like any schoolboy, the hero of the battlefield blushed and stammered in the presence of his associates. The artful speaker hastened to relieve the embarrassment which his own eulogy had aroused. "Sit down, Mr. Washington," said he. "Your modesty is equal to your valor, and that surpasses the power of any language that I possess."

When the session ended, Washington took his wife and her two children to Mount Vernon. There Mrs. Washington dispensed the hospitality of the home with all the grace for which Virginia ladies of the day were noted. The Marquis de Chastellux, a few years later, wrote of his visit there: "Your apartments were your home, the servants of the house were yours, and, while every inducement was held out to bring you into the general society of the drawing-room, or at the table, it rested with yourself to be served or not with everything in your own chamber."

Soon after his marriage Washington wrote to his kinsman, Richard Washington in London: "I am now, I believe, fixed in this seat with an agreeable partner for life, and I hope to find more happiness in retirement than I ever experienced in the wide and bustling world." Lossing describes him as "then twenty-seven years of age, over six feet two inches in height, and admirably proportioned. His hair was a rich dark-brown; his eyes grayish-blue and expressive of deep thought; his complexion florid; and his features regular and rather heavy.

"Washington's wife was three months younger than himself. She was a small, plump, elegantly-formed woman. Her eyes were dark and expressive of the most kindly good nature; her complexion fair; her features beautiful; and her whole face beamed with intelligence. Her temper, though quick, was sweet and placable, and her manners were extremely winning. She was full of life, loved the society of her friends, always dressed with a scrupulous regard to the requirements of the best fashions of the day, and was, in every respect, a brilliant member of the social circles which, before the Revolution, composed the vice-regal court at the old Virginia capital.

"Washington, at this time, possessed an ample fortune, independent of that of his wife. His estate at Mount Vernon he described as most pleasantly situated in 'a high, healthy country; in a latitude between the extremes of heat and cold, on one of the finest rivers in the world —a river well stocked with various kinds of fish at all seasons of the year, and in the spring with shad, herring, bass, carp, sturgeon, etc., in abundance. The borders of the estate,' he continued, 'are washed by more than ten miles of tide-water; several valuable fisheries appertain to it; the whole shore, in fact, is one entire fishery.' Such was the delightful home to which Washington took his bride in the spring of 1759."

At that time almost every manufactured article for

domestic use was imported from England. Two years after his marriage, Washington sent the following order to Robert Carey, Esq., in London:

For Master Custis, 8 Years Old

1   handsome suit of Winter Cloathes
A   suit of Summer ditto, very light
2   pieces Nankeens with trimmings
1   silver laced hat
6   pair fine Cotton Stockings
1   pr. fine worsted ditto
4   pr. Strong Shoes
1   pr. neat Pumps
1   pr. gloves
2   hair bags
1   piece ribbon for ditto
1   pr. silver Shoe and Knee buckles
1   p. Sleeve buttons
A   Small Bible neatly bound in Turkey, and John Parke
      Custis wrote in gilt letters on the inside of the cover
A   neat Small Prayer Book bound as above, with John
      Parke Custis, as above

Several items were ordered for a negro lad of fourteen, evidently young John Custis's body-servant; among them were:

3   pr. shoes for a boy 14 years old
3   pr. Coarse Stockings for do.
A   suit of livery Cloathes for the above boy of 14. A hat
      for do.

Note. Let the livery be suited to the arms of the Custis family.

For Miss Custis, 6 Years Old

A coat made of fashionable Silk
A fashionable Cap or Fillet with bib apron
Ruffles and Tucker—to be laced
4 fashionable dresses to be made of Long Lawn
2 fine Cambric frocks
A Sattin Capuchin hat and neckatees
A Persian quilted coat
1 pr. pack thread Stays
4 p. Calamanco Shoes
6 p. leather ditto and
2 p. Sattin do. with flat ties
6 pr. fine Cotton Stockings, 4 pr. White Wors'd Do.
1 pr. Silver Shoe buckles
1 pr. neat sleeve buttons
6 handsome Egrets different sorts
6 yds Ribbon Do.
1 pr. little Scissors
3 M (thousand) large pins. 3 M short whites
3 M minikens
1 Fashionable dressed Doll to cost a guinea. 1 Do. at 5s.
A box Gingerbread, Toys and Sugar Images, and Comfits
A neat Small Bible, bound in Turkey, and Martha Parke
    Custis wrote on the inside in gilt letters
A Small Prayer Book, neat and in the same manner
12 yards coarse green Callimanco
    The above things to be put into a Strong Trunk—separate from J. P. Custis's, whose will likewise be put into a Trunk, each having their names.
1 very good Spinet (a small harpsichord), to be made by Mr. Plinius, Harpsichord Maker, in South Audley Street, Grosvenor Square

It is begged as a favor that Mr. Carey would bespeak this

instrument as for himself or a friend, and not let it be known it is intended for exportation. Send a good assortment of spare strings to it.

Books according to the enclosed List—to be charged equally to both John Parke Custis and Martha Parke Custis —likewise one Ream of Writing paper.

"These specimens of orders sent annually to England," writes Lossing, "are given as glimpses of the domestic arrangements at Mount Vernon, and the style in which the wealthier Virginia families, of cultivated tastes, lived before the Revolution. It is evident that Washington and his family indulged in all the fashionable luxuries (not extravagances) of the day, pertaining to the table and the wardrobe; and in the absence of positive proof, these invoices would afford the strongest inferential evidences that they spent much of their earlier years in the enjoyment of social pleasures.

"Washington's diaries bear still stronger, because positive, testimony to the fact. During some months, two or three times a week, he records the result of a day's sport thus: 'Went a-hunting with Jacky Custis, and catched a fox, after three hours' chase. Found it in the creek.' Or, 'Mr. Bryan Fairfax, Mr. Grayson, and Phil. Alexander came home by sunrise. Hunted and catched a fox with these, Lord Fairfax, his brother, and Colonel Fairfax—all of them with Mr. Fairfax and Mr. Wilson of England, dined here.' Afterwards, two days in succes-cession: 'Hunted again with the same company.'

"Still more frequently he noted the arrival and departure of guests. One day the Fairfaxes, or Masons, or Thurstons, or Lees would be there; and the next day he and 'Mrs. Washington and Mr. and Miss Custis' would 'dine at Belvoir.' And so the round of visiting went on. The hunting day, which occurred so frequently, generally ended in a dinner at Mount Vernon or at Belvoir, a little lower on the Potomac—more frequently at the former; and the hospitalities of the house were kept up in a style which none but a wealthy planter could afford. 'Would anyone believe,' Washington says in his diary of 1768, 'that with a *hundred and one cows,* actually reported at a late enumeration of the cattle, I should still be obliged to buy butter for my family?'

"For Mrs. Washington and her lady visitors he kept a chariot and four horses, with black postillions in livery; and these were frequently seen and admired upon the road between Mount Vernon and Alexandria, or the neighboring estates. He took great delight in horses. Those of his own stable were of the best blood, and their names, as well as those of his dogs, were registered in his household books. When abroad, he always appeared on horseback; and as he was one of the most superb men and skillful horsemen in Virginia, he must have made an imposing appearance, especially when fully equipped for the road with the following articles, which were ordered by him from London, in one of his annual invoices:

1 Man's Riding-Saddle, hogskin seat, large plated stirrups, and everything complete. Double-reigned bridle and Pelham Bit, plated

A very neat and fashionable Newmarket Saddle-Cloth

A large and best Portmanteau, Saddle, Bridle, and Pillion Cloak-Bag Surcingle; checked Saddle-cloth, holsters, etc.

A Riding-Frock of handsome drab-colored Broadcloth, with plain double-gilt Buttons

A Riding Waistcoat of superfine scarlet cloth and gold lace with Buttons like those of the Coat

A blue Surtout Coat

A neat Switch Whip, silver cap

Black Velvet Cap for Servant

"Thus attired, and accompanied by Bishop, his favorite body-servant, in scarlet livery, Washington was frequently seen upon the road, except on Sunday morning, when he always rode in the chaise, with his family, to the church at Pohick or at Alexandria.

"Like other gentlemen living near the Potomac, Washington was fond of aquatic sports. He kept a handsome barge, which, on special occasions, was manned by black oarsmen in livery. Pleasant sailing-boats were frequently seen sweeping along the surface of the river, freighted with ladies and gentlemen going from mansion to mansion on its banks—Mount Vernon, Gunston Hall, Belvoir, and other places—on social visits.

"Washington and his wife frequently visited Annapolis and Williamsburg, the respective capitals of Maryland and Virginia. For fifteen consecutive years the Colonel was a member of the Virginia House of Burgesses, and Mrs. Washington spent much of her time with him at Williamsburg during the sessions. Both being fond of amusements, they frequently attended the theatrical representations there and at Annapolis. That form of entertainment was then a recent importation from England, the first company of actors, under the direction of Lewis Hallam, having performed in the

Maryland capital in 1752. Colonel and Mrs. Washington
also attended balls and parties given by the fashionable
people of Williamsburg and Annapolis, and frequently
joined in the dance.

"But it must not be supposed that during these years
of his earlier married life Washington's time was wholly,
or even chiefly, occupied in the pleasures of the chase
and of society. Far from it. He was a man of great
industry and method, and managed his large estates
with signal industry and ability. He did not leave his
farms to the entire care of his overseers. He was very
active, and continually, even when absent on public
business, exercised a general supervision of his affairs,
requiring a carefully prepared report of all operations
to be transmitted to him weekly, for his inspection and
suggestions.

"He was very abstemious, and while his table always
furnished his guests with ample and varied supplies for
their appetites, he never indulged in the least excess,
either in eating or drinking. He was an early riser, and
might be found in his library from one to two hours before daylight in winter, and at dawn in summer.

"Minutely journalizing his agricultural proceedings,
keeping his own accounts, making all his own surveys,
and, even before the Revolution, having an extensive
correspondence, Washington found much daily employment for his pen. The labors in his library, and a visit
to his stables, usually occupied the hours before breakfast. After making a frugal meal of Indian cakes, honey,
and tea or coffee, he would mount his horse and visit
every part of his estate where the current operations

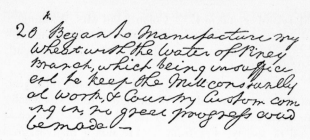

FACSIMILE OF AN ENTRY IN WASHINGTON'S DIARY

seemed to require his presence, leaving his guests to enjoy themselves with book and papers, or otherwise, according to their choice. He rode upon his farms entirely unattended, opening the gates, pulling down and putting up the fences, and inspecting, with a careful eye, every agricultural operation, and personally directing the manner in which many should be performed. Sometimes the tour of his farms, in the course of the morning might average twelve or fifteen miles; and on these occasions his appearance was exceedingly plain.

"His breakfast hour was seven o'clock in summer and eight in winter, and he dined at three. He always ate heartily, but was no epicure. His usual beverage was small beer or cider, and Madeira wine. He took tea and toast, or a little well-baked bread, early in the evening, conversed with or read to his family, when there were no guests, and usually, whether there was company or not, retired for the night at about nine o'clock.

"So carefully did Washington manage his farms that

they became very productive. His chief crops were wheat and tobacco, and these were very large—so large that vessels that came up the Potomac took the tobacco and flour directly from his own wharf, and carried them to England or the West Indies."

Upon his marriage Washington became the legal guardian of his two step-children, both of whom had been left amply provided for. No father ever showed more solicitude for his own children than did Washington for John and Martha Custis. To the management of their estates he gave the same care that he gave to his own. He kept a separate account for each child, and was scrupulous in crediting every penny accruing from the property. He was equally meticulous in charging to each child's account every article, however trifling, purchased for that child.

The personal supervision of the children Washington left, in the main, to their mother, who appears to have been very indulgent. That she spared the rod, contrary to the New England custom of the day, is plain. The family correspondence reveals the fact that Washington at times reasoned fervently and persistently, not only with John in his adolescence, but also with the son of John, whom he adopted.

John Parke Custis was placed under the tutelage of an Episcopal clergyman, the Reverend Jonathan Boucher, who exerted himself to make a scholar out of the pleasant lad, who loved a fox-hunt more than he did Euclid.

Martha, called "the dark lady," because of her complexion, was tenderly cared for at home. Her health

was never robust, and Washington secured for her all
the advantages which medical knowledge of the times
advocated. He took her to the "warm springs," in Virginia, but so far had the consumption progressed that
no lasting benefit was derived. During her last moments, her weeping family about her, Washington knelt
in prayer at her bedside.

We are told that after the death of her daughter,
Martha Washington became more indulgent than ever
to her son, John Parke Custis, then eighteen years old.
It is said that she often pleaded in his behalf "when
Washington found it necessary to exercise a wholesome
restraint upon him."

At about this time young John fell violently in love
with Eleanor, the second daughter of Benedict Calvert, of Mount Airy, Maryland, and much to the concern of Washington, when he discovered it, they formed
a matrimonial engagement. His only objection was their
extreme youth, but so strongly did he feel about it that
he addressed the following letter to Mr. Calvert:

"Mount Vernon, April 3rd, 1773.

"Dear Sir: I am now set down to write to you on a
subject of importance to you and of no small embarrassment to me. My son-in-law and ward, Mr. Custis, has,
as I have been informed, paid his addresses to your
second daughter, and having made some progress in
her affections, has solicited her in marriage. How far a
union of this sort may be agreeable to you, you best can
tell; but I should think myself wanting in candor were
I not to confess that Miss Nelly's amiable qualities are

acknowledged on all hands, and that an alliance with your family will be pleasing to his.

"This acknowledgment being made, you must permit me to add, sir, that at this, or in any short time, his youth, inexperience, and unripened education are, and will be, insuperable obstacles, in my opinion, to the completion of the marriage. As his guardian, I consider it my indispensable duty to endeavor to carry him through a regular course of education (many branches of which, I am sorry to add, he is totally deficient in), and to guard his youth to a more advanced age, before an event, on which his own peace and the happiness of another are to depend, takes place. Not that I have any doubt of the warmth of his affections, nor, I hope I may add, any fears of a change in them; but at present I do not conceive that he is capable of bestowing that attention to the important consequences of the married state which is necessary to be given by those who are about to enter into it, and of course I am unwilling he should do it till he is. If the affection which they have avowed for each other is fixed upon a solid basis, it will receive no diminution in the course of two or three years, in which time he may prosecute his studies, and thereby render himself more deserving of the lady, and useful to society. If, unfortunately, as they are both young, there should be an abatement of affection on either side, or both, it would better precede than follow marriage.

"Delivering my sentiments thus freely will not, I hope, lead you into a belief that I am desirous of breaking off the match. To postpone it is all I have in view; for I shall recommend to the young gentleman, with the warmth that becomes a man of honor (notwithstanding he did not vouchsafe to consult either his mother or me on the occasion), to consider himself as much engaged to your daughter as if the indissoluble knot were tied; and, as the surest means of effecting this, to apply himself closely to his studies (and in this advice, I flatter myself, you will join me), by which he will, in a great measure, avoid those little flirtations with other young ladies that may, by dividing the attention, contribute not a little to divide the affection.

"It may be expected of me, perhaps, to say something of property; but, to descend to particulars at this time must seem rather premature. In general, therefore, I shall inform you that Mr. Custis's estate consists of about fifteen thousand acres of land, a good part of it adjoining the city of Williamsburg, and none of it forty miles from that place; several lots in the said city; between two and three hundred negroes; and about eight or ten thousand pounds upon bond, and in the hands of his merchants. This estate he now holds, independent of his mother's dower, which will be an addition to it at her death; and, upon the whole, it is such an estate as you will readily acknowledge ought to entitle him to a handsome portion with a wife. But as I should never require a child of my own to make a sacrifice of himself to interest, so neither do I think it incumbent on me to recommend it as a guardian.

"At all times when you, Mrs. Calvert, or the young ladies can make it convenient to favor us with a visit, we should be happy in seeing you at this place. Mrs. Washington and Mr. Custis join me in respectful compliments, and,

"I am, dear sir, your most obedient servant,

"George Washington."

"It was agreed," says Custis, "that the youth should pass two years at college, before the marriage could take place. He was sent to King's (now Columbia) College, in New York City, but he remained there only a few months. Love and learning did not move in harmony, and on the third of February, 1774, young Custis was married to Miss Calvert, when the bridegroom was a little more than nineteen years of age."

The young couple had four children, the two younger of whom, on their father's early death, were adopted by Washington.

CHAPTER IV

THE CITIZEN PONDERS

Washington now proved as conscientious in the discharge of his civic duties as he had been ardent in his military activities on the frontier. He was a judge of Fairfax County, giving much personal attention and thought to his responsibilities in that office.

A member of the House of Burgesses for fifteen years, he was chosen by a large majority at each election. Here he mingled on terms of intimacy with substantial men of the colony, from burgesses to governor. This involved social amenities which were generously reciprocated at Mount Vernon, where such neighbors as George Mason of Gunston Hall, the Fairfaxes, including Sir Thomas, who now lived in his wilderness home, Greenway Court, the Carters, the Carlyles, and many others were constantly entertained. The names of Lewises, Washingtons, Bassetts, Dandridges, and others, to whom Washington and his wife were attached by ties of kinship, appear frequently on the pages of Washington's diaries.

Colonel Hugh Mercer, then in business at Fredericksburg as an apothecary, and Doctor James Craik, of Alexandria, both former comrades-in-arms, were often at Mount Vernon. Any veteran, whether officer or private, who had served with Washington, was always given a hearty welcome at his home.

"When he was at home," says Sparks, "a day seldom

passed without the company of friends or strangers at his house. In his diaries the names of these visitors are often mentioned, and we find among them the governors of Virginia and Maryland, and nearly all the celebrated men of the southern and middle colonies, who were afterwards conspicuous in the history of the country."

Washington and Mason probably continually weighed and discussed the measures of the British Parliament, which became more and more obnoxious to the Americans. The Stamp Act of 1764 was the cause of indignation throughout the colonies. Press and pulpit alike denounced it; and associations, called Sons of Liberty, were formed in every colony to oppose its enforcement.

It was the passage of this Act which evoked the eloquence of one of the modest members of the House of Burgesses. Patrick Henry had taken his seat in the house in the spring of 1765. The house was in session in the old capital at Williamsburg when news of the passage of the Stamp Act reached it. We are told that many angry comments were made privately, but none publicly until Henry, the youngest member of the Assembly, arose and offered a series of five Resolutions on the subject of the Act. The fifth Resolution declared that "the General Assembly of the colony have the sole right and power to levy taxes and impositions upon the inhabitants of this colony; and that every attempt to vest such power in any other person or persons whatsoever, other than the General Assembly aforesaid, has a manifest tendency to destroy British as well as American freedom."

According to Lossing, "A violent debate ensued, and Henry's genius was aroused in all its sublime majesty . . . His eloquence, like thunder-peals, shook that Assembly. In the midst of his harangue he summoned warning events from past history, and exclaimed, in clear bell-tones, 'Caesar had his Brutus, Charles the First his Cromwell, and George the Third ——' 'Treason!' cried the excited Speaker, Robinson; and 'Treason!' 'Treason!' resounded from every part of the house. Henry did not falter for a moment. Rising to a loftier altitude, and fixing his beaming eyes upon Robinson, he concluded his sentence with the words, 'may profit by their example. Sir, if this be treason, make the most of it!'

"When Henry was seated, Pendleton, Bland, Randolph, Wythe, and others, who afterwards became the boldest and most ardent opposers of British power, arose and denounced the Resolutions as disloyal, and dangerous to the public welfare. Their hearts were with the ardent Henry, but they adjudged his course to be premature and injudicious. Henry again took the floor, and his eloquence, like a mountain torrent, seemed to sweep before it every obstacle of opposition, and the Resolutions were adopted—the fifth by a majority of only one. During Henry's absence from the House the next day the Resolutions were reconsidered and modified, and the fifth—the soul of the whole—was stricken out. But manuscript copies were already on their way to other colonies, and the timidity of the Virginia Assembly did not soften their force.

"Previous to this time Washington seems not to have

expressed any positive opinion concerning the growing disputes between Great Britain and her colonies. Now, warmly sympathizing with his countrymen, he appears to have foreseen the inevitable struggle, and was preparing his mind for an active engagement in it. He no longer remained silent, yet he expressed his views with caution. Writing to Francis Dandridge, his wife's uncle, in London, he said: 'The Stamp Act imposed on the colonies by the Parliament of Great Britain engrosses the conversation of the speculative part of the colonists, who look upon this unconstitutional method of taxation as a direful attack upon their liberties, and loudly exclaim against the violation. What may be the result of this, and of some other (I think I may add, ill-judged) measures, I will not undertake to determine; but this I may venture to affirm, that the advantage accruing to the mother-country will fall greatly short of the expectations of the ministry; for certain it is that our whole substance already, in a manner, flows to Great Britain, and that whatsoever contributes to lessen our importations must be hurtful to her manufactures. The eyes of our people already begin to be open; and they will perceive that many luxuries, for which we lavish our substance, in Great Britain, can well be dispensed with, while the necessaries of life are mostly to be had within ourselves. This, consequently, will induce frugality, and be a necessary incitement to industry . . .

" 'As to the Stamp Act, regarded in a single view, one and the first bad consequence attending it is that our courts of judicature must inevitably be shut up; for it is impossible, or next to impossible, under our present circumstances, that the act of Parliament can be complied with, were we ever so willing to enforce its execution. And, not to say (which alone would be sufficient) that we have not money to pay for the stamps, there are many other cogent reasons which prove that it would be ineffectual. If a stop be put to our judicial proceedings, I fancy the merchants of Great Britain, trading to the colonies, will not be among the last to wish for a repeal of the Act.'

"The circular letter of the Massachusetts Assembly, proposing a colonial congress, met with a hearty response. Governor Fauquier, who was really opposed to the Stamp Act in principle, was, nevertheless, as the representative of the king, compelled to support it. Therefore, on being informed of the action of the Burgesses in adopting Henry's Resolutions, he dissolved the Assembly and ordered a new election, the result of which was highly satisfactory to the patriots. The eloquence of Henry seems to have touched every heart in the Old Dominion, and everywhere the people re-elected the friends of the Resolutions, and filled the seats of those opposed to them with undoubted patriots.

"Fauquier, perceiving the complexion of the new Assembly, refused to call the members together to appoint delegates to the proposed colonial congress. The members elect, confiding in the wisdom and patriotism of the delegates from the other colonies, signed a letter in which they promised to acquiesce in any action that might be had. Similar assurances were given by those of New Hampshire, North Carolina, and Georgia.

"The Colonial Congress assembled at New York, on

October 7, 1765, nine of the thirteen colonies being represented. The session continued fourteen days, and in three well-written documents, the grievances and rights of the colonists, a memorial to Parliament for a redress of the former, and an acknowledgment of the latter, and a petition to the king, were ably set forth. These proceedings were applauded by all of the provincial Assemblies, and when the first of November arrived (the appointed day for the Stamp Act to go into operation), the people were united in a strong determination to resist it. That day was observed as one of fasting and mourning. The colors of vessels were placed at half-mast. The courts were all closed; legal marriages ceased; ships remained in port; and, for a while, all business was suspended.

"There was quiet all over the land, but it was not the quiet of submission. It was only the ominous lull in the storm, which was to precede more furious blasts. The people were only gathering strength for more vigorous achievements in defense of their rights.

"Merchants entered into agreements not to import goods from Great Britain while the obnoxious Act remained a law; and in almost every family domestic manufactures were commenced. Everybody wore home-made clothing; and that wool might not become scarce, the use of sheep-flesh for food was discouraged. Very soon, from all classes in America, there went to the ears of the British ministry a respectful but firm protest. The merchants and manufacturers of London seconded it with great warmth, and thus made powerful, that voice was heard and heeded in high places.

"At about this time William Pitt appeared in Parliament as the earnest champion of the American. Then, also, Edmund Burke appeared on the same side; and during the stormy debates which ensued on the subject of repealing the Stamp Act, he achieved some of those earliest and most wonderful triumphs of oratory, which established his fame and endeared him to the American people.

"More powerful than oratory were the simple words of Benjamin Franklin, when he was examined before a committee of Parliament on the subject of the Stamp Act. He was asked, 'Do you think the people of America would submit to the stamp duty if it was moderated?'

" 'No, never,' replied Franklin, 'unless compelled by force of arms.'

" 'What was the temper of the American people before the year 1763?'

" 'The best in the world,' he answered. 'They submitted willingly to the government of the crown, and paid, in their courts, obedience to acts of Parliament. Numerous as the people are in the several old provinces, they cost you nothing in forts, citadels, garrisons, or armies, to keep them in subjection. They were governed by this country at the expense of only a little pen, ink, and paper; they were led by a thread. They had not only a respect, but an affection, for Great Britain; for its laws, its customs, and manners, and even a fondness for its fashions, that greatly increased the commerce. Natives of Great Britain were always treated with particular regard; to be an *Old England man* was, of itself, a character of some respect, and gave a kind of rank among us.'

"To the naturally succeeding question, 'And what is their temper now?' Franklin replied, 'Oh, very much altered.'

" 'Did you ever hear the authority of Parliament to make laws for America questioned till lately?' they asked.

" 'The authority of Parliament,' he replied, 'was allowed to be valid in all laws, except such as should lay internal taxes. It was never disputed in laying duties to regulate commerce.'

" 'If the Act is not repealed, what do you think will be the consequences?'

" 'A total loss of the respect and affection the people of America bear to this country, and of all the commerce that depends on that respect and affection,' Franklin firmly replied.

"Franklin's words were regarded as oracular, and these, with the voices from America, and from the British merchants and manufacturers, compelled the ministry to give way. The Stamp Act was repealed March 18, 1766, and that measure produced great joy in England and America. The warehouses of London were illuminated, and the shipping in the Thames was decorated with gay flags in testimony of satisfaction. In America public thanksgivings, bonfires, and illuminations attested the general joy. . . . A permanent reconciliation was anticipated.

"The repeal of the Stamp Act produced great satisfaction at Mount Vernon. 'The repeal,' wrote Washington to a friend, 'to whatever cause owing, ought much to be rejoiced at; for, had the Parliament of Great Britain resolved upon enforcing it, the consequences, I conceive,

would have been more direful than is generally appre-
hended, both to the mother country and her colonies.
All, therefore, who were instrumental in procuring the
repeal are entitled to the thanks of every British subject,
and have mine cordially.' "

It appears that the repeal of the Stamp Act was but
an expedient to allay the general discontent, for it was
preceded by a bill which declared that the king and
Parliament had the right to make laws, "to bind the
colonies and people of America, subjects of the crown of
Great Britain, in all cases whatsoever." This was called
the Declaratory Act, and we are told that it was passed
because it would insure the repeal of the Stamp Act.

Lossing says further: "While the eyes of the colonists
were filled with tears of joy because of the unexpected
repeal of the Stamp Act, they did not see the egg of
tyranny which lay concealed in the Declaratory Act.
Yet there were a few, like Gadsden of South Carolina,
who saw it clearly and hesitated not to declare the
public hopes to be fallacious. Washington, also, had
similar convictions. 'I cannot perceive,' he wrote to a
friend, 'what solid triumph of principle has been gained
by the repeal of the (Stamp) Act, while the tyrannical
power of Parliament is so strongly asserted. I rejoice
that the Act is repealed, because our people are spared
much trouble, and it is a concession to the popular will.
But I very much fear that out of the Declaratory Act
other oppressive measures will proceed, and that the
people of America will still be held in bondage if they
submit.'

"By another act Parliament required the colonial

Assemblies to provide, at the expense of the people, for troops that might be sent to America, with quarters, fire, beds, candles, beer, salt, and vinegar. The Massachusetts Assembly partially complied; but that of New York, pleading inability, begged to be excused from making the necessary appropriations. It was clearly perceived that a deep-laid scheme for enslaving the colonies, and drawing money from their coffers, was in progress, and that the advent of troops would be the introduction of a military despotism to enforce obedience to all laws, however obnoxious they might be to the Americans.

"The troops came from Halifax in June, 1766. They found a cool reception in Boston, and in New York their appearance was the signal for serious outbreaks. Parliament, by a large majority, proceeded to punish New York by suspending the powers of its governor and Assembly until they should comply with its requisitions concerning the troops. This served to strengthen the position of the recusant province, for it won the sympathy of all the other colonies. The Act created alarm and indignation all over the land, and the words of Richard Henry Lee, of Virginia, when he said, 'An Act for suspending the legislature of that province hangs like a flaming sword over our heads, and requires, by all means, to be removed,' found a warm and ready response in the hearts of the whole people.

"In June, 1767, a bill was passed for levying duties upon tea, glass, paper, painters' colors, etc., that should be imported into the colonies. Another bill became a law, early in July, which provided for the establishment of a board of trade in the colonies, independent of colonial legislation, and for creating resident commissioners of customs to enforce the revenue laws. Then, soon afterwards, the disabling Act concerning the New York Assembly, already mentioned, was passed. There was a provision in the Act relative to the quartering of troops in America, more odious than all others. In addition to the authorization of a standing army in the colonies, it enabled the crown, by sign manual, to establish a general civil list throughout every province, fixing the salaries of governors, judges, and other officers, such salary to be paid by the crown. Thus the executive and judicial officers, from whom the people were to expect good government, and the righteous administration of laws, were made entirely independent of the people, and became, in fact, mere hirelings of the crown.

"These direct blows at popular liberty, and these taxation schemes, produced an excitement in the colonies almost equal in intensity to that created by the Stamp Act. The colonial Assemblies uttered bold protests; new non-importation associations were formed; pamphlets, newspapers, and the pulpit put forth inflammatory appeals to the people, defining their rights and urging them to united resistance. Early in the year 1768 almost every colonial Assembly had spoken out boldly, and expressed its conviction that Parliament possessed no right to tax the colonies.

"The new commissioners of customs arrived in May, 1768, and they were regarded with great contempt, as instruments of oppression. The proceedings of the commissioners, on the arrival at Boston of a sloop belonging to the wealthy merchant, John Hancock, who was one of the popular leaders in Massachusetts, produced a serious outbreak, which resulted in the triumph of the popular will. The vessel was laden with Madeira wine. Payment of duties upon it was refused, and the commissioners seized the sloop. When the fact became generally known, a great concourse of citizens appeared, and speedily became a mob. They assailed the commissioners, damaged their offices, and dragging a customhouse boat through the town, they burned it upon the common. The commissioners, failing to receive aid or protection from the alarmed governor, fled for safety to Castle William, situated upon an island in the harbor, three miles from Boston, where a company of British artillery was stationed.

"Governor Bernard, perplexed by fear and indecision, unwisely invited General Gage, then in command of the British troops in America, to bring soldiers to Boston to overawe the inhabitants. When this invitation became known to the people, they were greatly irritated. A public meeting was held in Faneuil Hall, and James Otis, Samuel Adams, John Hancock, and John Adams were appointed to wait upon the governor and ascertain whether the report was true. The governor answered in the affirmative, but his usually haughty tone was changed to one of courtesy in the presence of those determined popular leaders. Mistaking the true character of those men, he attempted to bribe them by the gifts of social station. He presented Hancock with a commission as member of his council; that patriot tore the parchment into shreds in the presence of the people. He offered the lucrative place of advocate-general in the court of admiralty to

John Adams; the proffered patronage was rejected with disdain. The governor also approached that sturdy representative of the Puritans—that perfect model of disinterested patriotism—Samuel Adams, but found him, though poor in purse, as Hutchinson, on another occasion said, of such an obstinate and inflexible disposition that he could never be conciliated by any gift whatsoever.

"The engine of non-importation agreements, which worked so powerfully against the Stamp Act, was now put in motion with increased energy. During the winter and spring of 1769 these agreements, called *associations,* became general throughout the colonies, under the sanction of the Assemblies. Those who signed them were bound not to purchase or use the manufactures of Great Britain, and other goods usually exported from that country, except in cases of the most urgent necessity, during a specified time, unless the obnoxious laws were repealed.

"Just before the assembling of the Virginia legislature, in the spring of 1769, Washington received from Doctor Ross, of Bladensburg, in Maryland, sundry papers, which contained the Resolves and general proceedings of the merchants of Philadelphia, respecting these associations. On the fifth of April he communicated them to George Mason, his friend and neighbor, of Gunston Hall, and asked his opinion upon the subject. In his letter accompanying the package Washington declared his own sentiments with great energy and decision. 'At a time,' he wrote, 'when our lordly masters in Great Britain will be satisfied with nothing less than the deprivation of American freedom, it seems highly necessary that something should be done to avert the stroke, and maintain the liberty which we have derived from our ancestors. But the manner of doing it to answer the purpose effectually is the point in question. That no man should scruple, or hesitate a moment, to use arms in defense of so valuable a blessing is clearly my opinion. Yet arms, I would beg leave to add, should be the last resource, the *dernier resort*. We have already, it is said, proved the inefficacy of addresses to the throne and remonstrances to Parliament. How far, then, their attention to our rights and privileges is to be awakened or alarmed, by starving their trade and manufactures, remains to be tried.

" 'The northern colonies, it appears,' he continued, 'are endeavoring to adopt this scheme. In my opinion it is a good one, and must be attended with salutary effects, provided it can be carried pretty generally into execution. But to what extent it is practicable to do so, I will not take upon me to determine. That there will be a difficulty attending the execution of it everywhere, from clashing interests, and selfish, designing men, ever attentive to their own gain, and watchful of every turn that will assist their lucrative views, can not be denied; and in the tobacco colonies, where the trade is so diffused, and in a manner wholly conducted by factors for their principals at home (in England), these difficulties are certainly enhanced, but I think not insurmountably increased, if the gentlemen, in their several counties, will be at some pains to explain matters to the people, and stimulate them to cordial agreements to purchase none but certain enumerated articles out of any of the stores, after a definite period, and neither import nor purchase any themselves . . .

" 'The more I consider a scheme of this sort, the more ardently I wish success to it, because I think there are private as well as public advantages to result from it— the former certain, however precarious the other may prove. In respect to the latter, I have always thought that by virtue of the same power which assumes the right of taxation, the Parliament may attempt, at least, to restrain our manufactures, especially those of a public nature, the same equity and justice prevailing in the one case as the other, it being no greater hardship to forbid my manufacturing than it is to order me to buy goods loaded with duties, for the express purpose of raising a revenue.'

"After observing that extravagant and improvident living had impoverished many, very many, and caused the sale of a large number of estates for the benfit of creditors, Washington remarked: 'A scheme of this sort will contribute more effectually than any other that can be devised to extricate the country from the distress it at present labors under, I most firmly believe, if it can be generally adopted. And I can see but one class of people, the merchants excepted, who will not, or ought not, to wish well to the scheme, namely: they who live genteelly and hospitably on clear estates. Such as these, were they not to consider the valuable object in view, and the good of others, might think it hard to be curtailed in their living and enjoyments.

" 'Upon the whole, therefore, I think the scheme a good one, and that it ought to be tried here, with such alterations as our circumstances render absolutely necessary. But in what manner to begin the work is a matter worthy of consideration. Whether it can be attempted with propriety or efficacy, further than a communication of sentiments to one another, before May, when the general court and Assembly will meet at Williamsburg, and a uniform plan can be concerted, and sent into the different counties to operate at the same time, and in the same manner, everywhere, is a thing upon which I am somewhat in doubt, and I should be glad to know your opinion.'

"To this letter Mr. Mason replied the same day, at considerable length. 'I entirely agree with you,' he observed, 'that no regular plan of the sort proposed can be entered into here before the meeting of the general court at least, if not of the Assembly. In the meantime, it may be necessary to publish something preparatory to our gazettes, to warn the people of the impending danger, and induce them more readily and cheerfully to concur in the proper means to avert it; and something of this sort I had begun, but am unluckily stopped by a disorder which affects my head and eyes. As soon as I am able, I shall resume it, and then write you more fully or endeavor to see you. In the meantime, pray commit to writing such hints as may occur. Our all is at stake, and the little conveniences and comforts of life when set in competition with our liberty ought to be rejected, not with reluctance, but with pleasure . . . We may retrench all manner of superfluities, finery of all descriptions, and confine ourselves to linens, woolens, etc., not exceeding a certain price. It is amazing how much this practice, if adopted in all the colonies, would lessen the American imports, and distress the various traders and manufacturers in Great Britain. This would awaken their attention. They would see, they would feel, the oppressions we groan under, and exert themselves to procure us redress.'

"Not for a moment entertaining a thought of political separation from Great Britain, but evidently hoping for reconciliation, Mr. Mason continued: 'However singular I may be in my opinion, I am thoroughly convinced that, justice and harmony happily restored, it is not the interest of these colonies to refuse British manufactures. Our supplying our mother country with gross materials, and taking her manufactures in return, is the true chain of connection between us. These are the bands which, if not broken by oppression, must long hold us together, by maintaining a constant reciprocation of interest. Proper caution should, therefore, be used in drawing up the proposed plan of association. It may not be amiss to let the ministry understand that, until we obtain a redress of grievances, we will withhold from them our commodities, and particularly refrain from making tobacco, by which the revenue would lose fifty times more than all their oppressions could raise here.'

"Such were the sentiments of Washington and his compatriots in Virginia when they entered upon that long struggle for right, which resulted in the independence of the colonies."

CHAPTER V

THE CITIZEN AROUSED

In the brilliant group that assembled in Williamsburg in the spring of 1769, Washington was surrounded by men of such constructively patriotic ability and devotion as the country has seldom seen. Lossing's review of these personalities and the principles which they declared to an antagonistic Parliament is very interesting: "There was the bold Patrick Henry, whose trumpet-tones had recently awakened the moral echoes of a continent. There was Edmond Pendleton, the dexterous politician and graceful and persuasive speaker; and Richard Bland, the profound logician, eminent for the extent and accuracy of his knowledge. In the Speaker's chair was Peyton Randolph, the popular and eloquent leader of stern integrity and inflexible resolution, who presided over the first Continental Congress a few years later; and George Wythe, the simple, stern republican and elegant wit; and Richard Henry Lee, one of the most accomplished scholars and orators in America, who was called by common consent the Virginia Cicero. There, too, was Thomas Jefferson, a young lawyer, distinguished for his eminent abilities, liberality of views, and boldness of character, who now commenced his public life as a friend of mankind.

"The British Houses of Parliament had passed concurrent Resolves, censuring the votes, resolutions, and proceedings of Massachusetts. They also besought him (the king) to direct the governor of that province to send all persons 'charged with treason or misprision of treason' committed within that province since the thirtieth of December, 1767, to Great Britain for trial.

"When these Resolves reached the colonies, they created alarm and indignation. The governor of Massachusetts had dissolved the General Assembly of that province, and it had no legislature. Virginia promptly and generously took up the cause of Massachusetts. The Burgesses, by unanimous vote on the sixteenth of May, adopted a series of Resolutions, counter in letter and spirit to those of Parliament, and directed the Speaker forthwith to transmit them to all the houses of Assembly in America. In these Resolutions the doctrine that the sole right of imposing taxes on the inhabitants of a colony is vested in its Assembly; of the privilege of petitioning the sovereign for a redress of grievances; of the right of every accused person to a trial by his peers of the vicinage; and of the unconstitutionality of any law that should authorize the transportation to Great Britain of any colonial offender, for trial, was strongly put forth.

"This rebellious demonstration of the House of Burgesses greatly astonished and alarmed Lord Botetourt, the successor of the deceased Governor Fauquier. At noon the next day he suddenly appeared in the Assembly chamber during the session, and said: 'Mr. Speaker and Gentlemen, I have heard of your Resolutions and augur ill of their effects. You have made it my duty to dissolve you; and you are dissolved accordingly.'

"His lordship's action was expected by the Burgesses,

and their future course had been already determined. On the following morning they assembled in the Apollo room, at the Raleigh Tavern, when, professing to assume no other capacity than that of private citizens, they formed themselves into a voluntary convention, and appointed their late Speaker, Mr. Randolph, their moderator. When the convention was organized, Washington came forward and presented a draft of articles of association against the use of any merchandise imported from Great Britain, which had been concerted between himself and Mr. Mason. The association was signed by every person present, and copies were sent throughout the country for the signature of the people. These Burgesses then repaired to their respective counties, and were all re-elected.

"Washington adhered, with scrupulous exactness, to the terms of the association, and none of the proscribed articles were seen at Mount Vernon while it remained in force. In his first letter to his agent in London, after subscribing the association, he wrote: 'You will perceive, in looking over the several invoices, that some of the goods there required are upon condition that the act of Parliament imposing a duty on tea, paper, etc., for the purpose of raising a revenue in America, is totally repealed; and I beg the favor of you to be governed strictly thereby, as it will not be in my power to receive any articles contrary to our non-importation agreement, which I have subscribed, and shall rigidly adhere to, and should, if it were, as I could wish it to be, ten times as strict.' Hundreds of others in Virginia made the same cheerful sacrifice of luxuries, and even necessaries.

"Botetourt, wisely conforming his conduct to the demands of inexorable circumstances, conciliated the people, examined into alleged public grievances, and became a zealous advocate for a repeal of the laws so obnoxious to the colonists. When he died in 1771, the event was mourned by the Virginians as a public calamity.

"After these proceedings at Williamsburg, Washington's attention was called to the claims of the officers and soldiers in the late war, to lands in the Ohio country promised and granted to them in 1754 by an order in council and by the proclamation of Governor Dinwiddie. Early in 1770 immediate danger to their claims impended. A company in England solicited a grant, the proposed boundaries of which included nearly all the tract wherein lay the promised bounty-land. Washington at once took the matter in hand, as the champion of the soldier, with great zeal. He first laid before Lord Botetourt an historical account of the claim, and in a letter written on the fifteenth of April, 1770, he entered a warm protest against the proposed grant to the English company. 'I shall take the liberty,' he wrote, 'to inform your lordship that the bounds of that grant (solicited by Walpole and others), if obtained upon the extensive plan proposed, will comprehend at least four-fifths of the land, for the purchase and survey of which the government has lately voted two thousand five hundred pounds sterling. It must, therefore, destroy the well-grounded hopes of those (if no reservation is made in their favor) who have had the strongest assurances that the government could give, of enjoying a certain portion of the lands which have cost this country so much blood and treasure to secure.'

"Washington then cited the proposed boundary in detail, and added, 'These, my lord, are the bounds of a grant prayed for, and which, if obtained, will give a fatal blow, in my humble opinion, to the interests of this country.'

"He said in conclusion, 'These troops not only enlisted agreeably to the proclamation, but behaved so much to the satisfaction of the country as to be honored by the most public acknowledgment of it by the Assembly. Would it not be hard, then, my lord, to deprive men, under these circumstances, or these representations, of the just reward of their toils? Was not this act of the governor and council offered to the soldiers, and accepted by them, as an absolute compact? And though the exigency of affairs, or the policy of the government, made it necessary to continue these lands in a dormant state for a time, ought not their claim to be considered in preference to all others?'

"Washington's representations to the public authorities, and his untiring personal exertions, chiefly at his own cost, finally procured justice for the claimants. That nothing essential to their interests should remain undone, he resolved to visit the region under consideration and select the best tracts of land for his companions-in-arms. He set out from Mount Vernon on the fifth of October, 1770, accompanied by his friend and neighbor, Doctor Craik, and three negro attendants.

"Washington and his companions proceeded to Fort Pitt on horseback. After twelve days of wearying travel they were cordially received by Captain Edmondson, who commanded the little garrison. A town of twenty log houses had grown up, inhabited by Indian traders, and in one of them, while at dinner, Washington met his old acquaintance, George Croghan, who is said to have assisted him in carrying the wounded Braddock from the scene of his defeat, in 1755.

"At Croghan's residence, the next day, Washington was greeted by White Mingo and several other chiefs of the Six Nations, who remembered having seen him when he visited the French commander in 1753. A *'speech belt'* (wampum belt) was presented, which Washington accepted, and made a friendly reply.

"Washington and his companions left their horses at Fort Pitt and, accompanied by John Nicholson as interpreter, and William Crawford, a man well acquainted with the Indians, they descended the Ohio in a canoe to Point Pleasant, at the mouth of the Great Kanawha, a distance of two hundred and sixty-five miles.

"Although the voyage was one of great peril, all being ignorant of the channels of the river, and the real friendship of the Indians being a matter of much doubt, yet they had exquisite enjoyment for several days. Game abounded in great profusion, and Washington indulged in his favorite amusement of hunting to his heart's content. Floating upon the beautiful Ohio, they continually encountered large flocks of ducks and geese, while the branches of the trees which bent over the margins of the stream were filled with wild turkeys. Sometimes they would travel on foot for many miles through the forest, leaving the oarsmen in charge of the canoe. They examined the country and made valuable observations. In his field-book, Washington described the general contour of the country, the character of the soil as indicated by the nature of the trees, and the proximity of the streams to level tracts of land that might be eligible for settlements. They suffered severe hardships, for the weather became inclement, and they encamped at night with no other protection than their blankets.

"On the twenty-sixth of October the voyagers reached the hunting-camp of Kiashuta, the famous Seneca chief. Kiashuta immediately recognized Washington as the young ambassador whom he had seen seventeen years before at Venango. He received him in the most cordial manner, and after entertaining him and his party in the best of barbaric style, he assured Washington of his earnest desire to preserve everlasting peace between his people and the Virginians."

Washington and his party went on to the mouth of the Great Kanawha, where they remained two or three days engaged in marking such tracts of fine land in the vicinity as he intended to claim for the soldiers.

Doctor Craik afterwards related that while they were there, they were visited by an old chief who was a leader in the destruction of Braddock's troops on the field of Monongahela. He approached Washington with great reverence, at the head of several of his tribes, and addressed him through Nicholson, the interpreter, saying, as related by Custis: "I am a chief, and the ruler over many tribes. My influence extends to the waters of the great lakes and to the far blue mountains. I have traveled a long and weary path that I might see the young warrior of the great battle. It was on the day when the white man's blood mixed with the streams of our forest that

I first beheld this chief. I called to my young men and said, Mark yon tall and daring warrior? He is not of the red-coat tribe—he hath an Indian's wisdom, and his warriors fight as we do—himself is alone exposed. Quick, let your aim be certain, and he dies. Our rifles were leveled, rifles, which, but for him, knew not how to miss —'twas all in vain, a power mightier far than we shielded him from harm. He can not die in battle. I am old, and soon shall be gathered to the great council-fire of my fathers, in the land of shades, but ere I go, there is a something bids me speak, in the voice of prophecy. Listen! *The Great Spirit protects that man and guides his destinies—he will become the chief of nations, and a people yet unborn will hail him as the founder of a mighty empire!*"

Dr. Craik was highly entertained by the Indian's prophecy, and is said to have referred to it on a number of later occasions.

"Having ascended the Great Kanawha about fourteen miles and visited and examined every place he desired to, Colonel Washington and his party returned to Fort Pitt; with Doctor Craik and their servants he proceeded to Mount Vernon, where they arrived after an absence of nine weeks. He now pressed the matter of adjusting the soldiers' claims with great vigor, and finally, after much vexatious effort, he accomplished his object to the general satisfaction of all.

"There were a few exceptions. Colonel Muse, Washington's early military instructor, was dissatisfied and wrote an impertinent letter to Washington. It drew from the insulted colonel a most withering reply. The first paragraph is here quoted to show what a caustic pen Washington could wield when necessity called for its exercise: 'Sir: Your impertinent letter was delivered to me yesterday. As I am not accustomed to receive such, from any man, nor would have taken the same language from you personally, without letting you feel some marks of my resentment, I advise you to be more cautious in writing to me a second of the same tenor; for though I understand you were drunk when you did it, yet give me leave to tell you that drunkenness is no excuse for rudeness. But for your stupidity and sottishness, you might have known, by attending to the public gazette, that you had your full quantity of ten thousand acres of land allowed you.'

"Even Van Braam, who was suspected of treason at the Great Meadows, was not overlooked; he received nine thousand acres, which were subsequently purchased from him by Washington."

The echoes of the Boston Massacre, so-called, in 1770, reverberated to Virginia, where great sympathy was excited. Lord Dunmore was appointed governor of Virginia in place of the deceased Botetourt, and it is said that he appeared to value the character of Washington, calling on him for advice in the settlement of the claims of veterans to bounty lands.

"Lord Dunmore did not make Virginia his residence until in the summer of 1772. At that time the current of popular feeling in America against the imperial government was as strong as ever, but not so turbulent, for no event of sufficient importance to stir up the whole body of the colonists had recently occurred. But local disputes were irritating the people everywhere. In Virginia the efforts of legislators had been strongly put forth, for several years, to cast off the burden of negro-slavery from the province. We have already observed Thomas Jefferson rising into notice upon that topic, as the champion of emancipation. Again and again they had passed laws restraining the importation of negroes from Africa, but these enactments had always been disallowed by the higher authority; and in the year 1770 the king issued instructions, over his own signature, commanding the governor, 'upon pain of the highest displeasure, to assent to no law by which the importation of slaves should be in any respect prohibited or obstructed.'

"Yet the Virginians were not discouraged. They saw the light of hope in the future, and took heart. In April, 1772, the barbarous instructions of the king were freely debated in the Virginia Assembly, and the votes of Washington, Lee, Jefferson, Nicholas, Bland, Henry, and other patriots were cast for a resolution authorizing the transmission of an address to the king, in which they said: 'We are sensible that some of your Majesty's subjects in Great Britain may reap emoluments from this traffic; but when we consider that it greatly retards the settlement of the colonies with more useful inhabitants, and may, in time, have the most destructive influence, we presume to hope that the interest of a few will be disregarded, when placed in competition with the security and happiness of such numbers of your Majesty's dutiful and loyal subjects. Deeply impressed with these sentiments, we most humbly beseech your Majesty to remove all those restraints on your Majesty's governors of these colonies, which inhibit their assenting to such laws as might check so very pernicious a commerce.' The Virginians would not address Parliament on the subject, because that would be an acknowledgment of its right to interfere in their domestic concerns; so they made their appeal directly to the throne. It was unavailing, for the king's ear was now deaf to all reason from his transatlantic subjects.

"In other provinces the insolence of royal governors and subordinate servants of the crown was goading the people to rebellion, and their just indignation increased their boldness. In Virginia this spirit was everywhere manifested. The first measure of the Assembly, at its opening, after the arrival of Lord Dunmore, was an indication of the prevailing temper. The members, by resolution, demanded of his lordship by what authority he had awarded fees and salary to his secretary, to be paid out of the treasury of the province, without first consulting the Burgesses; and they wished to know whether his act was authorized by the crown. The governor, startled by this unexpected attitude of the Assembly, answered by wisely rescinding his order, for he perceived that the Virginians were deeply sympathizing with the inhabitants of Massachusetts in their opposition to a recent regulation of the ministry, by which the governor of the province was to receive his salary from the crown, and thus become independent of the people. Dunmore lost no time in proroguing an Assembly so untractable; and finding it continually unsubmissive to his control, he prorogued it from time to time, during several months. In the meanwhile he used every art to conciliate the members, but in vain, for he would not stoop from his aristocratic pedestal, nor yield a particle of his claimed prerogatives. At length circumstances compelled him to convene the Burgesses on the third of March, 1773.

"Washington was in his seat at the opening of the session. It was a short but a memorable one in the annals of the republic, for a measure of the greatest importance to the colonies was proposed and executed by the bold patriots of whom that Assembly was composed. The scheme had already assumed a tangible form in the minds of several of the members, for the proceedings of the Friends of Liberty in Boston had suggested it. That measure was the national system of committees of correspondence. In November previous Samuel Adams had arisen in a public meeting at Faneuil Hall and moved 'that a committee of correspondence be appointed, to consist of twenty-one persons, to state the rights of the colonists and of this province in particular as men, as Christians, and as subjects; to communicate and publish the same to the several towns in this province, and to the world, as the sense of this town, with the infringements and violations thereof that have been or from time to time may be made; also requesting of each town a free communication of their sentiments on this subject.' That motion was adopted, and a committee appointed, on which appear the names of James Otis, Samuel Adams, and Joseph Warren, names dear to every American citizen. The country quickly responded, and committees were soon organized in almost every town in the province.

"This was a bold step toward a confederation to resist further opposition. But Virginia speedily made a greater stride in that direction. On the second day of the session of the Burgesses just alluded to, the Assembly resolved itself into a committee of the whole house on the state of colony, when Dabney Carr, of Charlotte, brother-in-law of Jefferson, and a young man of brilliant genius and pure patriotism, moved a series of resolutions for a system of inter-colonial committees of correspondence. This measure had been concerted the evening previous at a caucus held in the Apollo room of the Raleigh Tavern at Williamsburg. That caucus consisted of Patrick Henry, Richard Henry Lee, Francis Lightfoot Lee, Thomas Jefferson, Dabney Carr, and two or three others. The Resolutions were written by Mr. Jefferson, and it was proposed that he should submit them to the House, but he preferred to give that honor to his youthful brother-in-law. The plan included a perfect union of all the colonies through committees of correspondence. It was, in effect, a proposition for a national confederation of the Anglo-American colonies. The eloquent voices of Patrick Henry, Peyton Randolph, and Richard Henry Lee were heard in favor of the Resolutions. But they needed no oral advocacy. They found a response in every patriot's heart. The whole Assembly approved of them and, on the twelfth of March, they were unanimously adopted, and a committee for Virginia was appointed.

"Massachusetts hailed these proceedings with delight, and a copy of the Virginia Resolutions was sent to every town and district in that province. Massachusetts had been the first to suggest committees of correspondence *within its own borders;* Virginia was the first to appoint a committee for *national* correspondence. Each colony seemed to have originated its particular scheme, notwith-standing the general idea was so similar; for, according to Peyton Randolph, the messengers from the respective legislatures, bearing the Resolutions of each, passed each other on the way.

"When the Resolutions just considered had been adopted by the Virginia Assembly, it proceeded to pass others equally unsubmissive in tone to arbitrary royal rule, when their proceedings were suddenly terminated by Governor Dunmore, who appeared in the legislative hall and proclaimed the dissolution of the Burgesses. They had already accomplished a great work, and were willing to return to their constituents as the faithful expo-nents of their principles. On the day succeeding the dis-solution of the Assembly, Washington journeyed home-ward on horseback in company with Richard Henry and Francis Lightfoot Lee, of Westmoreland, and Patrick Henry of Hanover. For a day and a half they traveled together; and no doubt those hopeful, earnest, and thoughtful patriots discussed long and solemnly the great question of the day: 'How long shall we submit to the oppressive policy of Great Britain?' That question was very soon answered by the inexorable logic of events.

"Early in 1773 a new thought upon taxation entered the brain of Lord North. The British East India Com-pany, having lost their valuable tea customers in Amer-ica by the operation of the non-importation associations, and having more than seventeen million pounds of the herb in their warehouses in England, petitioned Parlia-ment to take off the duty of three pence a pound, which was levied upon the article imported into the colonies.

Regarding it as a question of revenue, the company offered to pay the government more than an equal amount in export duty if the change should be made . . . But, blindly misapprehending the real question at issue, North introduced a bill into Parliament allowing the company to send their teas to America on their own account, without paying an export duty. As this would make tea cheaper in America than in England, the minister concluded that the colonists would not object to paying the three pence duty. This concession to a commercial monopoly, while the appeals of a great principle were spurned, was a new and aggravated offense, and created great indignation and contempt throughout the colonies.

"The East India Company, as blind as the minister, now regarded the American market as open for their tea, and soon after the passage of the bill they sent over several large ships laden with the article. The colonists had warned them that their adventure would be a loss, but North had assured them that the king was firm, and meant to try the question with the Americans. The latter were fully prepared for the issue.

"The people in the seaboard towns were informed of the approaching ships, and the consignees were known and marked. Almost at the same time, these vessels entered the harbors of Boston, New York, Philadelphia, Annapolis, Wilmington, and Charleston. Not a pound of any cargo was allowed to be sold. From some ports the ships left for England without removing their hatches; in others the tea was stored or destroyed. At Boston it led to a violent popular commotion. Two tea-ships were moored at a wharf, and the consignees, friends of Governor Hutchinson, acting under his advice, resolved to unload the vessels in spite of the menaces of the people. The inhabitants gathered daily in public meetings to discuss the matter, and to perform the duties of a monster vigilance committee. At length, on a cold moonlight evening in December, at the close of one of these meetings, at twilight, a large number of people, disguised as Indians, moving in concert according to a previous arrangement, boarded these vessels, broke open the hatches, and in the course of two hours shattered three hundred and forty-two chests of tea, and cast their contents into the waters of the harbor. Samuel Adams was one of the principal leaders in this movement; and the next morning the committee of correspondence appointed that inflexible patriot and four others to draw up a declaration of what had been done, to send forth to the world.

"The manly words of defense for the Americans, uttered by Burke and others, were unheeded, and Parliament, by enactment on the seventh of March, 1774, ordered the port of Boston to be closed against all commercial transactions whatever, and the removal of the customhouse, courts of justice, and other public offices, to Salem. The Salem people patriotically refused the proffered advantage at the expense of their neighbors; and the inhabitants of Marblehead, fifteen miles distant, offered the free use of their harbor and wharves to the merchants of Boston.

"Another Act became a law on the twenty-eighth of March, which leveled a deadly blow at the charter of

Massachusetts. It decreed that all counselors, judges, and magistrates should be appointed by the crown, and hold office during the royal pleasure. Thus they became paid instruments of oppression.

"A third retaliatory Act was passed on the twenty-first of April, providing for trial in England of all persons indicted in the colonies for murder, or other capital offense, committed in aiding the magistracy; giving, as Colonel Barré said on the floor of the House of Commons, 'encouragement to military insolence already so insupportable.'

"A fourth Bill, providing for the quartering of troops in America, was also passed, by large majorities in both houses of Parliament.

"These oppressive measures, condemned alike by the voice of expediency and common humanity, were speedily put in operation. The Boston Port-Bill was to take effect on the first of June. Intelligence of its passage had produced alarm and indignation in the doomed town, and the inhabitants prepared to meet their sad fate with fortitude.

"The people of all the colonies made common cause with the Bostonians. The blow about to be inflicted upon that city might fall, at any time, elsewhere, and the liberties of all were in jeopardy. That blow had weakened the last link of colonial fidelity. The desire for political independence began to kindle in many hearts and thrilled their nerves like an electrical stream, making the recipients prophetic. They saw in the present little hope for reconciliation, for the standpoints of argument of the contestants were widely different.

"Peyton Randolph, the Speaker of the House of Burgesses, received a letter from the Massachusetts committee of correspondence, announcing the passage of the bill for closing the port of Boston on the first of June and for inflicting other injuries upon that unhappy town. Randolph read the letter to the House when in full session, and at its close a general murmur of indignation spread over the Assembly, followed by bold and eloquent denunciation of the measure. A strong protest against that and the other retaliatory measures of Parliament was entered upon the journal, and on the twenty-fourth the House adopted a resolution of condolence with their persecuted sister colony, and passed an order, setting apart the first day of June as a day of fasting, humiliation, and prayer 'to implore the Divine interposition for averting the heavy calamity which threatened destruction to their civil rights, and the evils of civil war, and to give them one heart and one mind firmly to oppose, by all just and proper means, every injury to American rights.' At noon the following day, while the members were engaged in an animated debate, they were summoned to the council chamber by Lord Dunmore, who addressed them as follows: 'Mr. Speaker, and Gentlemen of the House of Burgesses: I have in my hand a paper, published by order of your House, conceived in such terms as reflect highly upon his Majesty and the Parliament of Great Britain, which makes it necessary for me to dissolve you, and you are dissolved accordingly.'

"The delegates, eighty-nine in number (among whom was Washington), immediately reassembled in the Apollo room, at the Raleigh Tavern, organized themselves into a voluntary convention, and prepared an address to their constituents, in which they declared, 'that an attack made on one of our sister colonies, to compel submission to arbitrary taxes, is an attack made on all British America, and threatens ruin to the rights of all, unless the united wisdom of the whole be applied.' They also recommended the committee of correspondence to communicate with the several committees of the other colonies, on the expediency of appointing deputies to meet annually in a general congress to deliberate on such measures as the united interests of the several colonies might require.

"So, almost simultaneously and without concert, Virginia and Massachusetts made a similar proposition to the people of America, of the greatest importance, and prepared to act upon it. The Massachusetts Assembly immediately appointed five delegates to attend a general congress when it should assemble, but the Virginians postponed further action on the subject until a more convenient time. The proposition met with a hearty response from the other colonies, and it was agreed that a general congress of delegates should meet at Philadelphia on the fifth of September ensuing.

"At dawn, on the first of June, the day on which the port of Boston was to be closed, the bells of Brenton church, of the capitol, and of William and Mary college tolled solemnly, for it was the appointed day for fasting, humiliation, and prayer. Religious services were held in Brenton church, and Washington noted in his diary at evening: 'June 1st, Wednesday. Went to church and fasted all day.' Every true patriot in Williamsburg and vicinity who could attend was there, and the church was crowded. On the following day most of the delegates departed for their homes, but Washington was detained by business and did not leave for Mount Vernon until the twentieth. During all the interval his friendly relations with Dunmore and his family continued, and they parted with mutual expressions of good-will.

"General Gage, the commander-in-chief of all the British forces in America, was appointed to succeed Hutchinson as governor of Massachusetts, in order to enforce the Port-Bill and the other arbitrary enactments of Parliament, and toward the close of April he prepared to leave New York to take possession of his new office.

"He landed at Long Wharf on the thirteenth of May, and found the people very much excited, for they had just received intelligence of the passage of the Port-Bill.

"The cause of Boston became the cause of all the colonists, and the active sympathies of the people abroad were commensurate with the sufferings of the patriots of that town, when their harbor was closed, their business crushed, and destitution sat in every place. The rich, deprived of their rents, became straitened, and the poor, denied the privilege of labor, were reduced to beggary. But help came to the patriots there in the hour of their need from every colony.

"No hope of reconciliation appeared, and the people, persuaded that war was inevitable, began to arm themselves and practice military tactics daily. The fife and drum were heard everywhere; and fathers and sons, encouraged by the gentler sex, took lessons together in the art of war. The forge and hammer were busy in making guns and swords, and everything bore the animated but gloomy impress of impending hostilities. During the summer and autumn the people of New England enrolled themselves into military companies, and prepared to take up arms at a minute's warning. Such was the origin of the famous 'minute-men,' whose blood was poured out at Lexington, and Concord, and Bunker Hill.

"In other colonies, especially in Virginia, the spirit of liberty now waxed strong, and the forms of resistance multiplied daily. Soon after Washington's return to Mount Vernon meetings were held in the several colonies, pursuant to the recommendation of the circular issued from Williamsburg. At these meetings Resolutions expressive of the sentiments of the people were adopted, and delegates to the convention to be held at Williamsburg, on the first of August, were elected. Washington presided at the meetings in Fairfax County, and was appointed one of a committee to prepare a series of resolutions concerning the late acts of Parliament, the rights of the colonies, and the proper course to be pursued by them, and to report the same, at a meeting to be held at the courthouse, on the eighteenth of July."

These resolutions were the famous Fairfax County Resolves, doubtless drawn up by George Mason. They reiterated and emphasized the feelings of the patriots with regard to the obnoxious acts of Parliament. Washington was appointed to present these Resolves to the convention at Williamsburg on the first of August, 1774.

Up to this time, though attending all meetings and serving on all important committees, Washington had been one of the more silent members of every assemblage. Content to aid in the furtherance of all patriotic measures, he left oratory to such men as Patrick Henry, Peyton Randolph, and others more gifted than himself.

It was on the occasion of presenting the Fairfax Resolves to the convention at Williamsburg that he broke the habit of years, and gave utterance to what Mr. Lynch, of South Carolina, pronounced "the most eloquent speech that ever was made." Washington's address was brief, but one sentence of it has proved unforgettable to this day. He declared, with feeling, "I will raise one thousand men, subsist them at my own expense, and march, myself at their head, for the relief of Boston."

Patrick Henry's estimate of Washington is doubtless a true one. Sparks relates that Henry, soon after his return from the Congress, was asked whom he thought the greatest man in that body. He replied, "If you speak of eloquence, Mr. Rutledge of South Carolina is by far the greatest orator; but if you speak of solid information and sound judgment, Colonel Washington is unquestionably the greatest man on that floor."

CHAPTER VI

THE COMMANDER-IN-CHIEF

We now follow Washington to Philadelphia at the beginning of September, in 1774. He left Mount Vernon on horseback on the last day of August in company with Patrick Henry and Edmund Pendleton, who had been his guests there. The rate of travel in those days being limited to the capacity of horsepower, it was not until the fourth of September that Washington wrote in his diary, "Lodged at Doctor Shippen's, in Philadelphia, after supping at the New Tavern."

On Monday, September fifth, the delegates to the Congress met in Carpenters' Hall. Lossing describes the meeting-place and details the procedure of the assemblage. "The assembly-room in that building, some forty-five feet square, had been chosen for the meeting-place. In the chamber above was quite a fine library belonging to the Carpenters' Association; and a pleasant lobby afforded a place for walking and conversation. On the question, 'Are you satisfied with this room?' being put, it was answered in the affirmative.

"Thomas Lynch, of South Carolina, who was a member of the Stamp Act congress in 1765, arose and said: 'There is a gentleman present who has presided with great dignity over a very respectable society, greatly to the advantage of America, and I therefore propose that the Honorable Peyton Randolph, Esquire, one of the delegates from Virginia, and the late Speaker of the House of Burgesses, shall be appointed chairman. I doubt not the choice will be made by unanimous vote." And so it was; and Mr. Randolph, a large, good-looking man, forty-five years of age, took the chair and opened the preliminary proceedings with great dignity.

"Mr. Lynch again arose and proposed that Mr. Charles Thomson (who was then present on the invitation of some delegates to take minutes of the proceedings) should be chosen the permanent secretary. Thomson was chosen, and he at once entered upon the duties of that important office, which he discharged with singular ability and fidelity for almost fifteen years. The gentlemen from the several colonies now presented their respective credentials, which were read and approved; and before noon the immortal Continental Congress was organized and solemnly inaugurated as a national deliberative assembly.

"The men who composed that first Congress were possessed of the purest minds, the loftiest and most disinterested patriotism, and moral characters without spot or blemish. The people seemed instinctively to have turned to their best men for counsel and action when the crisis arrived; and the representatives there assembled composed the flower of the American colonies. John Adams wrote, 'There is in this Congress a collection of the greatest men upon this continent, in point of abilities, virtues, and fortunes.' In the opinion of Charles Thomson no subsequent Congress during the war could compare with the first in point of talent and purity.

"The credentials of the several delegates having been

read, Mr. Duane, of New York, moved the appointment
of a committee to prepare regulations for the Congress,
when the question arose, 'What shall be the method of
voting? By colonies, by the poll, or by interest?' Then
came a pause. Who should take the lead? They had
come together from distant provinces, some instructed
by the power that appointed them, others left free to act
as circumstances should require. The silence was profound. It was becoming painful, when a grave-looking
member in a plain, dark suit of minister's gray, and un-
powdered hair, arose. 'Then,' said Bishop White, who
was present and related the circumstance, 'I felt a regret
that a seeming country parson should have so far mistaken his talents and the theater for their display.' But
his voice was so musical, his words so eloquent, and his
sentiments so profoundly logical that the whole house
was electrified. The question, 'Who is it? Who is it?'
went from lip to lip. A few who knew the speaker, answered, 'It is Patrick Henry, of Virginia!' There was
no more hesitation. From that hour the great business
of the Congress moved on."

It was not until the second day of their deliberations
that the assemblage acted on the motion of Mr. Cushing
that the Congress should be opened with prayer. "Mr.
Jay and Mr. Rutledge opposed the motion because the
delegates were so divided in religious sentiments that they
could not join in the same act of worship. Mr. Samuel
Adams rose, and said: 'I am no bigot, and can hear a
prayer from a gentleman of piety and virtue, who is, at
the same time, a friend to his country. I am a stranger
in Philadelphia, but have heard that Mr. Duché deserves

that character, and, therefore, I move that Mr. Duché, an Episcopal clergyman, be desired to read prayers to the Congress tomorrow morning.' The motion was seconded and passed in the affirmative.

"Mr. Duché accepted the invitation of Congress to open the session on the morning of the seventh with prayer, and at the appointed hour 'he appeared with his clerk, and in his pontificals,' as John Adams wrote to his wife. . . . When, after reading several prayers, Mr. Duché turned to the appointed psalm for the seventh day of the month, its appropriateness on that occasion was very marked, and the effect of the reading of it was powerful. It was the thirty-fifth psalm, in which David thus prays for protection against his enemies:

Plead my cause, O Lord, against them that strive with me, and fight against them that fight against me.

Take hold of shield and buckler, and stand up for mine help.

Draw out also the spear, and stop the way against them that persecute me; say unto my soul, I am thy salvation . . . .

"All hearts present warmly responded 'Amen' to the supplications of that psalm. 'I never saw a greater effect upon an audience,' wrote John Adams to his wife. 'It seemed as if Heaven had ordained that psalm to be read on that morning. After this, Mr. Duché unexpectedly struck out into an extempore prayer, which filled the bosom of every man present. Episcopalian, as he is, Dr. Cooper himself never prayed with such fervor, such ardor, such earnestness and pathos, and in language so eloquent and sublime for America, for Congress, for the province of Massachusetts Bay, and especially for the town of Boston. It has had an excellent effect upon everybody here.' Bishop White, who was present, says that Washington was the only delegate present who knelt during these prayers, that being the custom of Episcopalians, other denominations standing on such occasions."

The next day John Adams wrote to his wife concerning the Resolutions: "They were passed in full Congress, with perfect unanimity. The esteem, the affection, the admiration for the people of Boston and the Massachusetts, which were expressed yesterday, and the fixed determination that they should be supported, were enough to melt a heart of stone. I saw the tears gush into the eyes of the old, grave, pacific Quakers of Pennsylvania." On the day of the adoption of the Resolutions Adams wrote to his wife, "This was one of the happiest days of my life. In Congress we had generous, noble sentiments and manly eloquence. This day convinced me that America will support the Massachusetts or perish with her."

About a month later the Congress gave a whole day to the consideration of a letter from Massachusetts and the adoption of the resolution: "That this Congress approve the opposition of the inhabitants of Massachusetts Bay to the execution of the late acts of Parliament; and if the same shall be attempted to be carried into execution by force, in such case, all America ought to support them in their opposition."

Surely John Adams rejoiced again. Washington at about this time received a letter from Captain Robert Mackenzie, an old friend and comrade-in-arms, who wrote thus: "The rebellious and numerous meetings of men in arms, their scandalous and ungenerous attacks upon the best characters in the province, obliging them to save themselves by flight, and their repeated but feeble threats to dispossess the troops, have furnished sufficient reasons to General Gage to put the town in a formidable state of defense, about which we are now fully employed, and which will be shortly accomplished to their great mortification."

Washington replied, expressing his pleasure that Mackenzie intended to visit him at Mount Vernon, and continued: "Permit me, with the freedom of a friend (for you know I always esteemed you), to express my sorrow that fortune should place you in a service that must fix curses to the latest posterity upon the contrivers, and, if success (which, by-the-bye, is impossible) accompanies it, execrations upon all those who have been instrumental in the execution . . . I conceive that when you condemn the conduct of the Massachusetts people, you reason from effects, not causes; otherwise you would not wonder at a people, who are every day receiving fresh proofs of a systematic assertion of arbitrary power, deeply planned to overthrow the laws and constitution of their country, and to violate the most essential and valuable rights of mankind."

At the close of the congressional session Washington retired to Mount Vernon, though continuing to follow closely the course of events. The long-suffering patriots of Massachusetts at length convened in a provincial Congress, electing John Hancock their president. This Congress appointed a committee of safety, with John Hancock at its head, delegating to it general executive powers and right of calling out the militia of the province. Another commitee was appointed to provide arms, ammunition, and stores, for which purpose upward of sixty thousand dollars were appropriated. Provision was also made for the general arming of the minute-men of the province. Artemas Ward, Jediah Preble, and Seth Pomeroy were commissioned as generals. Henry Gardner was chosen treasurer of the colony, with the title of receiver-general.

"These proceedings of the Congress," says Lossing, "were generally approved throughout the province. Ammunition and stores were speedily collected at Concord, Woburn, and other places. Mills were erected for mak· ing gunpowder; manufactories of arms were established. . . . The army of twelve thousand was soon increased to twenty thousand, with John Thomas and William Heath commissioned as additional generals.

"This army, strong, determined, generous, and panting for action, was invisible to the superficial observer. It was not seen in the camp, the field, nor the garrison. No drum was heard calling it to action. It was like electricity, harmless when latent, but terrible when aroused. It was all over the land. It was at the plow, in the workshop, and in the counting-room. Almost every household was its headquarters and every roof its tent. It bivouacked in every chamber; and mothers, sisters, wives, and sweethearts made cartridges for its muskets and supplied its commissariat.

"The flame of rebellion that burst out in New England spread southward. In the middle provinces the

people were seen everywhere in the practice of military
discipline. Virginia, with its quick ear, had early caught
the sound of martial preparations; and when Washington returned to Mount Vernon, he found the independent companies throughout the province waiting for the
voice of his experience to teach them how to prepare for
the conflict.

"A few days after his arrival the Independent Company of Cadets of Prince William County, a well-
appointed corps, solicited him to take command of them
as field officer. Other companies offered him the same
honor; and throughout the province, when the people felt
that war with the mother country was inevitable, they
turned, as with one heart and mind, to Washington. He
yielded to these solicitations and reviewed the troops
which assembled at various places; and much of the
winter of 1774-1775 was spent by him in this important
service."

The events at Lexington, Concord, and Ticonderoga
had taken place before the second Continental Congress
convened at Philadelphia on May 10, 1775. At this meeting it was unanimously resolved "That the doors be kept
shut during the time of business, and that the members
consider themselves under the strongest obligations of
honor to keep the proceedings secret, until the majority
shall direct them to be made public."

Congress proceeded to adopt the armed forces raised
"or to be raised for the defense of the colonies" as the
American Continental army. It was later resolved that
"a general be appointed to command all the continental
forces, raised or to be raised, for the defense of American

liberty"; and "that five hundred dollars per month be allowed for the pay and expenses of the general." The selection of a general was next considered. John Adams, in an eloquent and impressive address, emphasized all the high qualifications needful in the discharge of so fateful a command. George Washington, in the uniform of a colonial colonel, was an attentive listener to the delegate from Massachusetts. When the general remarks of the speaker became more personal and he announced his intention to propose for the office a gentleman from Virginia, a member of the Congress, Washington rose from his seat and left the room, perhaps overcome by the same emotion that embarrassed him when publicly thanked for his frontier services by the House of Burgesses.

We may safely conclude that the gravity of the events into which Washington was thus drawn called forth reserves of strength and poise which made him forever afterwards absolute master of himself in any contingency. The few notable exceptions were such as to elicit the admiration and affection of those around him.

Washington accepted the command of the army, not upon the terms of the Congress, but upon terms characteristic of his self-sacrificing patriotism. He agreed to serve for the duration of the hostilities without remuneration except for current expenses.

In the letter to his wife informing her of his appointment to the command of the army he designates it as "a kind of destiny that has thrown me upon this service" and hopes "that my undertaking it is designed to answer some good purpose."

Writing to his brother, John Augustine, he said: "I shall hope that my friends will visit and endeavor to keep up the spirits of my wife as much as they can, for my departure will, I know, be a cutting stroke upon her; and on this account alone I have many disagreeable sensations. I hope that you and my sister, though the distance is great, will find so much time this summer as to spend a little at Mount Vernon."

Washington did not return to Mount Vernon, but left Philadelphia on the twenty-first of June for Cambridge, to take command of the army, "not doubting" as he wrote to his wife, "but I shall return safe to you in the fall."

A troop of light-horse escorted him to Cambridge, and as they neared Trenton they met a courier riding in haste to inform Congress of the battle of Bunker Hill. Washington's anxious inquiry, on hearing the news, was, "How did the militia behave?" Being informed of their steadfastness and bravery, he exclaimed, "Then the liberties of the country are safe!" and proceeded with confirmed optimism.

His progress was marked with the greatest interest and enthusiasm. In Boston he was remembered by some who had met him twenty years before, when as a young colonel he had appealed to Shirley for redress of certain grievances. All were eager now to see their Commander-in-chief, and people congregated for a glimpse of him. His presence and bearing excited universal admiration.

Doctor Thacher, a surgeon in the army, wrote in his military journal, "I have been much gratified this day with a view of General Washington. His Excellency was on horseback, in company with several military gentlemen. It was not difficult to distinguish him from all others; his personal appearance is truly noble and majestic, being tall and well proportioned."

Mrs. John Adams wrote to her husband, "I was struck with General Washington. You had prepared me to entertain a favorable opinion of him, but I thought the half was not told me. Dignity, with ease and complacency, the gentleman and soldier, look agreeably blended in him. Modesty marks every line and feature of his face." The lady even quoted Dryden in describing him, setting a fashion which still endures.

Mercy Warren, wife of the president of the provincial Congress, writing of Washington, Lee, and Gates, said: "The first of them I think one of the most amiable and accomplished gentlemen, both in person, mind, and manners, that I have met with."

Officers and men were attracted to him and became his lifelong supporters in spite of the indefinable dignity which repelled familiarity and inspired many with feelings akin to awe when in his presence.

CHAPTER VII

PECULIAR DIFFICULTIES

It became apparent, soon after Washington's formal installation as commander-in-chief, that opposition to the enemy was only one, and perhaps the least vexatious and heartbreaking, of the many difficulties that beset him. It is not intended in these pages to follow the course of every campaign, but rather to indicate the events and circumstances which throw the clearest light upon his many-sided personality.

Always regarding himself merely as the servant of the American people, he was in constant communication with Congress from the very first. Immediately acquainting himself with the condition and strength of his own army, as well as the disposition of the enemy, he reviewed the whole in a long letter to Congress, closing as follows: "My best abilities are at all times devoted to the service of my country, but I feel the weight, importance, and variety of my present duties too sensibly not to wish a more immediate and frequent communication with the Congress. I fear it may often happen, in the course of our present operations, that I shall need that assistance and direction from them which time and distance will not allow me to receive."

When Washington assumed command of the Colonial forces, he found himself confronted with the task of co-ordinating groups of men from all walks of life, many of them born and bred in the sturdy independence of rural occupations. The description of the patriots before the battle of Bunker Hill, contained in Kidder's *History of New Ipswich,* describes the forces in general. It is from an eye-witness. "To a man, they wore small-clothes, coming down and fastening just below the knee, and long stockings, with cowhide shoes ornamented by large buckles, while not a pair of boots graced the company. The coats and waistcoats were loose and of huge dimensions, with colors as various as the barks of oak, sumach, and other trees and shrubs of our hills and swamps could make them. Their shirts were all made of flax, and like every other part of the dress, were home-made. On their heads were worn large, round-top, and broad-brimmed hats. Their arms were as various as their costume; here an old soldier carried a heavy Queen Anne's musket, with which he had done service in the conquest of Canada, many years before, while by his side walked a stripling with a Spanish fusee, not half its weight or caliber, which his grandfather may have taken at the Havana; while not a few had old French pieces, which dated back to the siege of Louisburg. Instead of a cartridge-box, a large powder-horn was slung under the arm, and occasionally a bayonet might be seen bristling in the ranks. Some of the swords of the officers had been made by our province blacksmiths, perhaps from some farming utensil, and appeared serviceable, but heavy and uncouth."

The testimony of the Reverend William Emerson, of Concord, Massachusetts, a chaplain of one of the regiments, indicates the same diversity not only in accouterments, but in the hastily-contrived shelter, doubtless erected by individuals according to their tastes or abilities. "Who would have thought," wrote Chaplain Emerson, "twelve months past, that all Cambridge and Charlestown would be covered over with American camps and cut up into forts and intrenchments, and all the lands, fields, and orchards laid common—horses and cattle feeding in the choicest mowing land, whole fields of corn eaten down to the ground, and large parks of well-regulated locusts (locust-trees) cut down for firewood and other public uses? This, I must say, looks a little melancholy. My quarters are at the foot of the famous Prospect Hill, where such preparations are made for the reception of the enemy. It is very diverting to walk among the camps. They are as different in their form as the owners are in their dress, and every tent is a portraiture of the temper and taste of the persons who encamp in it. Some are made of boards, and some of sail-cloth; some partly of one and partly of the other. Again, others are made of stone or turf, brick or brush. Some are thrown up in a hurry; others are curiously wrought with doors and windows, done with wreaths and withes, in the manner of a basket. Some are your proper tents and marquees, looking like the regular camp of the enemy. In these are the Rhode Islanders, who are furnished with tent-equipage and everything in the most exact English style. However," adds the discerning divine, "I think this great variety rather a beauty than a blemish in the army."

Writing to his friend, Richard Henry Lee, of Virginia, at Philadelphia, Washington expressed his determination as well as a measure of apprehension: "Between you and me, I think we are in an exceedingly dangerous situation, as our numbers are not much larger than we suppose those of the enemy to be, from the best accounts we are able to get. . . . The abuses in the army, I fear, are considerable, and the new modeling of it, in the face of an enemy, from whom we every hour expect an attack, is exceedingly difficult and dangerous. If things, therefore, should not turn out as the Congress would wish, I hope they will make proper allowances. I can only promise and assure them that my whole time is devoted to their service, and that as far as my judgment goes, they shall have no cause to complain."

Congress at this time was attempting to establish systematic civil government as well as to make provision for the army. A postal system was established, to extend "from Falmouth, in New England, to Savannah, in Georgia," with Benjamin Franklin at its head. At the same time a committee was appointed to "make inquiry in all the colonies after virgin lead and leaden ore, and the best methods of collecting, smelting, and refining it."

Proceeding in grand style, Congress voted five hundred thousand dollars to be sent to Washington for the use of the army at Boston.

An army hospital to accommodate twenty thousand men was planned, and Doctor Benjamin Church was placed at its head. Dr. Church had been considered so brave and zealous a patriot by Warren and his associates that he had been admitted to their most secret deliberations, even at a time when it was apparent that the enemy was receiving information from within the most trusted circles. He had frequently taken the required oath not to divulge the nature of the proceedings of the Sons of Liberty and other groups. Following soon upon his appointment as Surgeon General to the Continental army he was detected in carrying on a secret correspondence with General Gage. After being tried by a court-martial, Dr. Church was found guilty of correspondence with the enemy. He was expelled from the general Assembly of Massachusetts, and confined in jail at Norwich, Connecticut. Because of failing health, however, he was released and allowed to leave the country. He sailed for the British West Indies, but the vessel on which he took passage was lost at sea.

One of Washington's first acts was to organize his army in three grand divisions, composed of six brigades of six regiments each. By this arrangement every colony's troops were commanded by an officer of that colony, so far as possible. This tactful measure was designed to allay petty jealousies that might arise from pretensions to rank.

Owing to an error on the part of the committee of supplies, Washington soon found himself embarrassed by a great scarcity of powder, a state of affairs which continued to hamper him, from time to time, throughout the war.

He was distressed to learn of the imprisonment, in the common jail in Boston, of American officers captured by the British on Bunker Hill. Being a former comrade-in-arms of General Gage, with whom he had served under Braddock, he wrote a courteous protest to Gage "that no consideration has been had for those of the most respectable rank when languishing with wounds and sickness."

Gage replied haughtily, "Your prisoners, whose lives, by the laws of the land, are destined to the cord, have hitherto been treated with kindness and more comfortably than the king's troops in the hospitals—indiscriminately, it is true, for I acknowledge no rank that is not derived from the king."

Upon receipt of this letter Washington ordered all British prisoners then on parole at Watertown and Cape Ann to be confined in Northampton jail, without distinction of rank. He took pains to explain to them that the reason for this treatment was dictated by their own general. However, he directed his secretary, Colonel Joseph Reed, to write to the committee of Northampton, while the British prisoners were on their way there, to request that the captives should be allowed to go about upon their parole immediately upon their arrival. Colonel Reed added, "The General further requests that every other indulgence and civility consistent with their security be shown to them, so long as they demean themselves with decency and good manners. As they have committed no hostility against the people of this country, they have a just claim to mild treatment; and the General does not doubt that your conduct toward them will be such as to compel their grateful acknowledgment that Americans are as merciful as they are brave."

Washington, in his instructions to Colonel Benedict Arnold, included the following paragraph, numbered 10: "If Lord Chatham's son should be in Canada, and in any way fall into your power, you are enjoined to treat

him with all possible deference and respect. You cannot
err in paying too much honor to the son of so illustrious
a character, and so true a friend to America. Any other
prisoners who may fall into your hands, you will treat
with as much humanity and kindness as may be consistent with your own safety and the public interest. Be
very particular in restraining, not only your own troops,
but the Indians, from all acts of cruelty and insult,
which will disgrace the American arms and irritate our
fellow-subjects against us."

General Schuyler, having arrived at Ticonderoga,
wrote to Washington, apprizing him of conditions there.
"You will expect," he wrote, "that I should say something
about this place and the troops here. Not one earthly
thing for offense or defense has been done. The commanding officer had no orders; he only came to reinforce
the garrison, and he expected the general (Schuyler).
But this, as well as what follows in this paragraph, I
pray may be *entre nous,* for reasons I need not suggest.
About ten last night I arrived at the landing place, the
north end of Lake George; a post occupied by a captain
and one hundred men. A sentinel, on being informed
that I was in the boat, quitted his post to go and awake
the guard, consisting of three men, in which he had no
success. I walked up and came to another, a sergeant's
guard. Here the sentinel challenged, but suffered me to
come up to him; the whole guard, like the first, in
soundest sleep. With a penknife, only, I could have cut
off both guards, and then have set fire to the block-
house, destroyed the stores, and starved the people here.
At this post I had pointedly recommended vigilance and

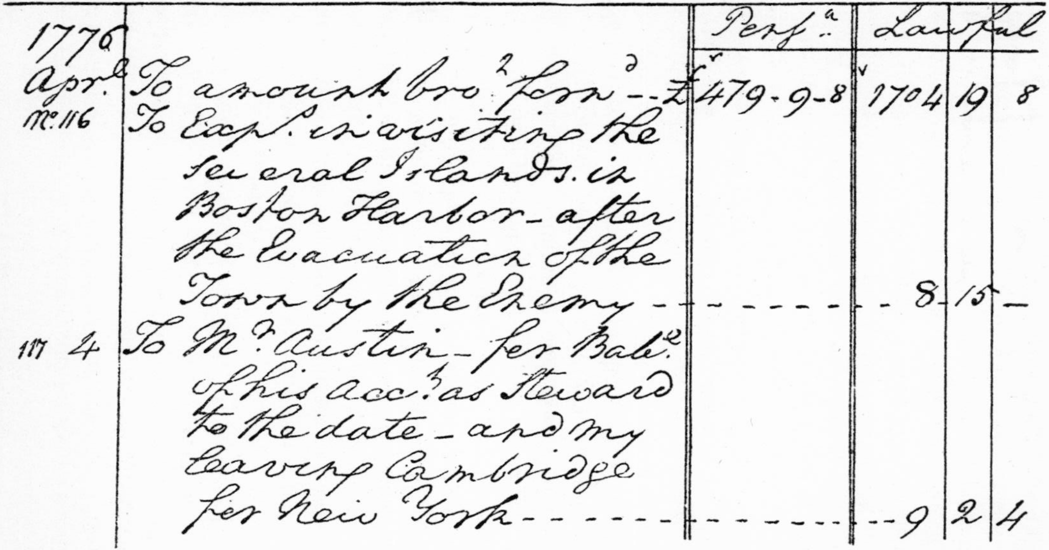

		Perf.a	Lawful		
1776 Aprl.	To amount bro.t forw.d -- £	479-9-8	1704	19	8
No. 116	To Exps. in visiting the several Islands in Boston Harbor — after the Evacuation of the Town by the Enemy ----------		8	15	—
117 4	To Mr. Austin — per Bal.e of his acc.t as Steward to the date — and my leaving Cambridge for New York ----------		9	2	4

FACSIMILE OF A PART OF WASHINGTON'S EXPENSE ACCOUNT WITH THE UNITED STATES care, as all stores for Fort George must necessarily be landed there. But I hope to get the better of this inattention. The officers and men are all good-looking people, and decent in their deportment, and I really believe will make good soldiers, as soon as I can get the better of this nonchalance of theirs. Bravery, I believe, they are far from wanting."

Washington replied, expressing his sympathy: "I can easily judge of your difficulties in introducing order and discipline into troops, who have, from their infancy, imbibed ideas of the most contrary kind. It would be far beyond the compass of a letter for me to describe the situation of things here on my arrival. Perhaps you will only be able to judge of it from my assuring you that mine must be a portrait at full length of what you have had in miniature. Confusion and discord reigned in every department, which, in a little time, must have ended either in the separation of the army or fatal contests with one another. . . . However, we mend every day, and I flatter myself that in a little time we shall work up these raw materials into a good manufacture. I must recommend to you, what I endeavor to practice myself, patience and perseverance."

The patience, but not the perseverance, of Washington was strained when he felt obliged to write to Congress, just three months after taking command, as follows: "It gives me great pain to be obliged to solicit the attention of the honorable Congress to the state of this army, in terms which imply the slightest apprehension of being neglected. But my situation is inexpressibly distressing, to see the winter fast approaching upon a naked army, the time of their service within a few weeks of expiring, and no provision yet made for such important events. Added to these, the military chest is totally exhausted; the paymaster has not a single dollar in hand; the commissary general assures me he has strained his credit, for the subsistence of the army, to the utmost. The quartermaster general is in precisely the same situation; and the greater part of the troops are in a state not far from mutiny, upon the deduction from their stated allowance. I know not to whom I am to impute this failure; but I am of opinion, if the evil is not immediately remedied, and more punctuality observed in future, the army must absolutely break up. I hoped I had so fully expressed myself on this subject, both by letter and to those members of the Congress who honored the camp with a visit, that no disappointment could possibly happen. I therefore hourly expected advices from the paymaster that he had received a fresh supply."

The rearrangement of the army into twenty-six regiments instead of the former thirty-eight gave Washington and his advisers much anxiety. The task was one which required the greatest tact, as well as judgment and firmness. On the eleventh of November Washington dispatched a letter to the president of Congress. "The trouble I have in the arrangement of the army is really inconceivable," he wrote. "You, sir, can much easier judge than I can express the anxiety of mind I must labor under on the occasion, especially at this time, when we may expect the enemy will begin to act on the arrival of their reinforcement, part of which is already come, and the remainder daily dropping in."

It was Washington's strong desire to foster a spirit of unity among the troops, by the creation of a *continental,* rather than a *colonial* army. In this he seems to have had great difficulty, as expressed in a letter to Colonel Reed: "Connecticut wants no Massachusetts man in their corps; Massachusetts thinks there is no necessity for a Rhode Islander to be introduced into hers; and New Hampshire says it is very hard that her valuable and experienced officers, who are willing to serve, should be discarded, because her own regiments, under the new establishment, cannot provide for them." In this matter Washington was bound by the decisions of the committee of conference. However, such were the difficulties in enlisting men that, after a month's intensive effort, only about five thousand recruits had been obtained.

Commenting on the situation, Washington wrote to Colonel Reed at the close of November: "Such a dearth of public spirit, and such want of virtue, such stock-jobbing, and fertility in all the low arts to obtain advantage of one kind or another, in this great change of military arrangement, I never saw before, and pray God's mercy that I may never be witness to again. What will be the end of these maneuvers is beyond my scan. I tremble at the prospect. We have been till this time enlisting about three thousand five hundred men. To engage them I have been obliged to allow furloughs as far as fifty men to a regiment, and the officers, I am persuaded, indulge in as many more. The Connecticut troops will not be prevailed upon to stay longer than their time, saving those who have enlisted for the next campaign, and are mostly on furlough; and such a mercenary spirit pervades the whole that I should not be at all surprised at any disaster that may happen. In short, after the last of this month our lines will be so weakened that the minute-men and militia must be called in for their defense; and then, being under no kind of government themselves, will destroy the little subordination I have been laboring to establish, and run me into one evil whilst I am endeavoring to avoid another. Could I have foreseen what I have experienced, and am likely to experience, no consideration upon earth should have induced me to accept this command. A regiment or any subordinate department would have been accompanied with ten times the satisfaction, and, perhaps, the honor."

A letter from General Greene to Ward, the deputy-governor of Rhode Island, intimates that Washington was likely to modify his opinion after closer acquaintance with his men. Speaking of Washington, Greene wrote: "He has not had time to make himself acquainted with the genius of this people. They are naturally as brave and spirited as the peasantry of any other country, but you cannot expect veterans of raw militia from only a few months' service. The common people are exceedingly avaricious; the genius of the people is commercial, from their long intercourse with trade. The sentiment of honor, the true characteristic of a soldier, has not yet got the better of interest. His Excellency has been taught to believe the people here a superior race of mortals; and finding them of the same temper and dispositions, passions and prejudices, virtues and vices of the common people of other governments, they sank in his esteem."

Although Washington relieved his feelings by expressing himself forcibly, it was in strictest confidence, and no hint of this feeling was allowed to circulate. A stern front of bold determination was consistently presented to the enemy, not only by Washington and his officers, but also by those in government circles.

Benjamin Franklin, writing to his friend Doctor Priestley, in England, said, at about this time: "Tell our dear, good friend, Doctor Price, who sometimes has his doubts and despondencies about our firmness, that America is determined and unanimous; a very few tories and placemen excepted, who will probably soon export themselves. Britain, at the expense of three millions, has killed one hundred and fifty Yankees this campaign, which is twenty thousand pounds a head; and at Bunker Hill she gained a mile of ground, half of which she lost again by our taking post on Ploughed Hill. During the same time sixty thousand children have been born in America. From these data his mathematical head will easily calculate the time and expense necessary to kill us all and conquer our whole country."

It might be difficult to ascertain whether the good philosopher's figures were obtained from official vital statistics or were conjured by his own lively brain in an optimistic moment, but his humor subtly conveys a suggestion of the spirit which pervaded the colonies.

Nevertheless, Washington continued to beseech his friends to aid him in overcoming the incomprehensible obstacles which hampered him at every turn. Writing to Richard Henry Lee, he said, "For God's sake, hurry up the signers of money, that our wants may be supplied."

The treatment of American prisoners by the British

continued to distress Washington. About the middle of December he was informed of the capture, after a brave resistance, of Colonel Ethan Allen. Allen had not surrendered without the assurance of honorable treatment for himself and his small surviving force, seven of whom were wounded. The Americans had been delivered to General Prescott, then in command at Montreal, who proceeded to abuse them in an angry tirade, calling Allen a rebel and vowing dire vengeance. The captives had been confined in the hold of the schooner "Gaspé," the soldiers fastened together in pairs with handcuffs, and an eight-foot bar of iron riveted to Allen's shackles. Allen had written to Prescott as follows, but had received no response:

"Honorable Sir: In the wheel of transitory events I find myself prisoner, and in irons. Probably your Honor has certain reasons, to me inconceivable, though I challenge an instance of this sort of economy of the Americans during the war to any officers of the crown. On my part, I have to assure your Honor that when I had the command and took Captain Delaplace and Lieutenant Fulton, with the garrison at Ticonderoga, I treated them with every mark of friendship and generosity, the evidence of which is notorious even in Canada. I have only to add that I expect an honorable and humane treatment, as an officer of my rank and merit should have, and subscribe myself your Honor's most obedient servant."

Washington, on receipt of this information, wrote to General Howe* on the eighteenth, demanding his im-

* Prescott had in the meantime been taken by the Americans.

mediate intercession, saying: "From the character which Mr. Howe bears as a man of honor, gentleman, and soldier, I flatter myself that my demand will meet with his approbation. I take the liberty, also, of informing you that I shall consider your silence as a confirmation of the report; and further assuring you that whatever treatment Colonel Allen receives, whatever fate he undergoes, such, exactly, shall be the treatment and fate of Brigadier General Prescott, now in our hands."

Howe, although disclaiming jurisdiction in the matter to Washington in haughty terms, nevertheless wrote the following day to Lord Dartmouth, saying: "Mr. Washington, presuming upon the number and rank of the prisoners in his possession, has threatened retaliation in point of treatment to any prisoners of theirs in our power." This threat of Washington's secured for Allen, upon his arrival in England, more lenient treatment than would otherwise have been accorded him.

The operations of Dunmore in Virginia, such as his plan to incite the Indians against the inhabitants, his promise to free all slaves who would desert their patriotic masters (by which many deluded negroes were left without care or protection of any kind), and his inhuman destruction of Norfolk, all caused Washington great anxiety.

In this connection, Lund Washington,* to whom was entrusted the management of Washington's farms, wrote to the General: "Many people have made a stir about Mrs. Washington's continuing at Mount Vernon, but I cannot think there is any danger. The thought, I be-

---

* Kinsman and friend of Washington.

lieve, originated in Alexandria; from thence it got to Loudoun, and I am told the people of Loudoun talk of sending a guard to conduct her up to Berkeley, with some of their principal men to persuade her to leave this place, and accept their offer. Mr. John Augustine Washington wrote pressing her to leave Mount Vernon. She does not believe herself in danger. Lord Dunmore will hardly himself venture up this river; nor do I believe he will send on that errand. Surely, her old acquaintance, the attorney who, with his family, is on board his ship, would prevent his doing an act of that kind. You may depend I will be watchful, and upon the least alarm persuade her to remove."

Washington wrote to his wife, asking her to join him at headquarters, which she proceeded to do. Accompanied by her son, John Parke Custis, and his young wife, she made the long journey from Mount Vernon in a coach drawn by four blooded horses, driven and accompanied by postillions in the family scarlet-and-white livery, to which were added various complimentary escorts from place to place. Arrived at Cambridge, she became the central figure in much pleasant entertaining, not only in military circles, but in the social life of the community. The staid New Englanders experienced an enlivening Christmas cheer in the circle which moved about the charming Virginia lady and her family.

Mrs. Washington's zeal for the common cause was attested by her wardrobe. Two of her dresses which were of great interest to the New England ladies were of cotton striped with silk. She confessed that they were entirely home-made, the silk stripes in the fabric having been woven from the ravelings of brown silk stockings and old crimson damask chair-covers. She said also that she had a great deal of domestic cloth made in her home, sixteen spinning-wheels being kept in constant operation.

Many traditions of Mrs. Washington's gentle kindness were cherished in military circles. She is said to have occupied herself, even when entertaining or when herself the recipient of hospitality, in knitting warm hose and gloves, which she distributed among the young men of her husband's military family.

Dr. Thacher, after dining with General Washington and his wife at the winter encampment, writes of Mrs. Washington in his journal: "This lady combines in an uncommon degree great dignity of manner with the most pleasing affability, but possesses no striking marks of beauty. I learn from the Virginia officers that Mrs. Washington has ever been honored as a lady of distinguished goodness, possessing all the virtues which adorn her sex, amiable in her temper and deportment, full of benignity, benevolence, and charity, seeking for objects of affection and poverty, that she may extend to the sufferer the hand of kindness and relief."

Of General Washington Dr. Thacher writes, on the same occasion: "His tall and noble stature and just proportions, his fine, cheerful, open countenance, simple and modest deportment, are all calculated to interest every beholder in his favor, and to command veneration and respect. He is feared even when silent, and beloved even while we are unconscious of the motive . . . In conversation his Excellency's expressive countenance is peculiarly interesting and pleasing; a placid smile is frequently observed on his lips, but a loud laugh, it is said, seldom, if ever, escapes him. He is polite and attentive to each individual at table, and retires after the compliment of a few glasses."

It may be that while Mrs. Washington was at winter quarters, she reminded her husband of those unfortunate neighbors at home who depended upon his bounty; for the General wrote to Lund Washington as follows: "Let the hospitality of the house, with respect to the poor, be kept up. Let no one go hungry away. If any of this kind of people should be in want of corn, supply their necessities, provided it does not encourage them in idleness; and I have no objection to your giving my money in charity, to the amount of forty or fifty pounds a year, when you think it well bestowed. What I mean by having no objection is, that it is my desire that it should be done. You are to consider that neither myself nor wife is now in the way to do these good offices. In all other respects I recommend it to you, and have no doubt of your observing, the greatest economy and frugality; as I suppose you know that I do not get a farthing for my services here, more than my expenses. It becomes necessary, therefore, for me to be saving at home."

The news that Montreal was in the possession of Montgomery brightened the military horizon, and supplies for the necessities of the soldiers were received. These cheering influences stimulated enlistments, and the outlook for the coming year seemed in general more satisfactory.

CHAPTER VIII

INCREASING DIFFICULTIES

The year 1776, far from diminishing the apprehensions, though never the resolution and steadfastness, of Washington, seems to have brought to him the same annoying limitations with which he had struggled on taking command. While pleading for the necessary armaments with which to take the offensive, he was compelled to remain passive in the face of public clamor for action. To Colonel Reed he wrote in February: "I know the unhappy predicament in which I stand. I know that much is expected of me. I know that without men, without arms, without ammunition, without anything fit for the accommodation of a soldier, little is to be done. And, what is mortifying, I know that I cannot stand justified to the world without exposing my own weakness and injuring the cause by declaring my wants, which I am determined not to do, farther than unavoidable necessity brings every man acquainted with them. My situation is so irksome to me at times that if I did not consult the public good more than my own tranquillity, I should, long ere this, have put everything on the cast of a die. So far from having an army of twenty thousand men well armed, etc., I have been here with less than half that number, including sick, furloughed, and on command, and these neither armed nor clothed as they should be. In short, my situation has been such that I have been obliged to use art to conceal it from my own officers."

That the situation was not concealed entirely is evinced by a letter written from Boston by Colonel Moylan, during a period of unusually mild weather. "The bay is open," wrote the colonel, "and everything thaws here, except Old Put.* He is still as hard as ever, crying out for powder! Ye gods, give us powder!"

However, all the restraints imposed by lack of powder were insufficient to cause Washington to waver in his fixed determination to see his country freed from oppressive government. Commenting upon a speech of the king he wrote to Colonel Reed, "I would not be deceived by artful declarations or specious pretenses; nor would I be amused by unmeaning propositions; but in open, undisguised, and manly terms . . . I would tell them (the British) that the spirit of freedom beat too high in us to submit to slavery, and that if nothing else would satisfy a tyrant and his diabolical ministry, we were determined to shake off all connection with a state so unjust and unnatural. This I would tell them, not under cover, but in words as clear as the sun in its meridian brightness."

That this spirit was not confined to Washington is indicated by a letter written by General Nathanael Greene. Concerning the same message of the king, Greene wrote: "He breathes revenge and threatens us with destruction. America must raise an empire of permanent duration, supported from the grand pillars of truth, freedom, and religion, based upon justice, and defended by her own

---

* General Israel Putnam.

patriotic sons." In another letter, Greene wrote to a
member of Congress: "Permit me to recommend from
the sincerity of my heart, ready at all times to bleed
in my country's cause, a *declaration of independence;*
and call upon the world, and the great God who governs
it, to witness the necessity, propriety, and rectitude
thereof."

With the eventual evolution and adoption of the
Declaration thus advocated by Greene and Washington,
we are familiar.

Perhaps anticipating the ebullition which followed
the reading of the *Declaration* to the assembled army in
New York, Washington, in his orders for the day, had
said: "The general hopes and trusts that every officer
and man will endeavor so to live and act as becomes a
Christian soldier, defending the dearest rights and liberties of his country." He rebuked as riotous and unbecoming the overthrow of the leaden statue of George
the Third, but he heartily approved its later conversion
into bullets for the use of his army.

To the conflict of armies was now added the conflict
of personalities. From the very first, General Horatio
Gates improved every smallest opportunity to exalt himself at the expense of others. Beginning these tactics
with respect to General Schuyler, he later applied them
to Washington.

Another troublesome character, of whom Washington at first expected great things, was Major General
Charles Lee. Lee was an Englishman by birth, who came
to America in command of a company of grenadiers,
and engaged in the French and Indian war. At the out-

break of the American Revolution he was the seasoned veteran of several foreign campaigns and noted for courage and skill. He professed great sympathy with the cause of the colonists and gladly accepted the honor of being chosen one of the four major generals of the Continental army in June, 1775. His acceptance of the honor, however, was contingent upon a pledge from Congress that he should be indemnified for any losses he might sustain in consequence of his participation in the conflict. Congress made a solemn pledge of such indemnity, the only one of its kind ever requested.

It was not until the winter of 1776, however, in the course of the operations in New Jersey, that Lee began that systematic disobedience and frustration of Washington's most explicit orders, which at length culminated in his own downfall. At the same time he began a steady, malicious detraction, causing even Colonel Joseph Reed, of Philadelphia, to waver in his loyalty to the Commander-in-chief, who had taken him into his most sacred confidence in numerous letters.

It was in December of 1776 that Lee wrote to Gates, with whom he seemed to be in perfect accord: "The ingenious maneuver of Fort Washington has completely unhinged the good fabric we have been building. There never was so damned a stroke; *entre nous,* a certain great man is most damnably deficient. He has thrown me into a situation where I have my choice of difficulties; if I stay in this province I risk myself and army; if I do not stay, the province is lost forever . . . Our counsels have been weak to the last degree. As to what relates to yourself, if you think you can be in time to aid the

General, I would have you, by all means, go. You will, at least, save your army."

This letter was barely signed when Lee, in dressing-gown and slippers, was taken prisoner by the enemy. The British were generally greatly elated, but when the word reached Sir Joseph Yorke, who knew Lee well, he is reported to have said, "He is the worst present any army can receive."

In military circles Washington consistently deplored Lee's loss. To his brother he wrote: "You will undoubtedly have heard of the captivity of General Lee. This is an additional misfortune, and the more vexatious, as it was by his own folly and impudence, and without a view to effect any good that he was taken."

The personnel of the Congress having declined, people were beginning to lose confidence in that body. Following the Declaration of Independence some of Congress's members had been withdrawn for civil service to their respective states; others were serving in the army, and their places had been filled with men of inferior quality. Probably no one felt this change more than Washington, hampered as he was by their ineptitude; but even at this time, when the public treasury was exhausted and the credit of the country had utterly vanished, he did not lose hope. Speculations being the fashion as to what would happen if Philadelphia, then the seat of government, should be taken, he resolutely replied: "We will retreat beyond the Susquehanna River; thence, if necessary, to the Allegheny Mountains. Numbers will repair to us for safety, and we will try a predatory war. If overpowered, we must cross the Alleghenies."

However, Congress being compelled to flee from Philadelphia, they bestirred themselves to replenish the public treasury and passed a resolution to the effect that "until the Congress shall otherwise order, General Washington shall be possessed of full power to order and direct all things relative to the department and the operations of war."

Thus armed with the powers of a military dictator, Washington felt able to achieve something more immediately effective than crossing the Alleghenies, as the events of Trenton and Princeton testify.

That Washington knew how to make the most of every situation and had the courage and resolution to wrest victory from the most adverse circumstances was forcibly demonstrated, not only at Trenton, but also at Princeton. His personal courage in the face of danger was manifested in every engagement in which he took part, but never more impressively than at Princeton. It is here retold by Custis.

"The heroism of Washington on the field of Princeton is matter of history. We have often enjoyed a touching reminiscence of that ever-memorable event from the late Colonel Fitzgerald, who was aid to the Chief, and who never related the story of his General's danger and almost miraculous preservation, without adding to his tale the homage of a tear.

"The aid-de-camp had been ordered to bring up the troops from the rear of the column, when the band under

General Mercer became engaged. Upon returning to
the spot where he had left the Commander-in-chief, he
was no longer there, and, upon looking around, the aid
discovered him endeavoring to rally the line which had
been thrown into disorder by a rapid onset of the foe.
Washington, after several ineffectual efforts to restore
the fortunes of the fight, is seen to rein up his horse,
with his head to the enemy, and in that position to become immovable. It was a last appeal to his soldiers,
and seemed to say, Will you give up your general to the
foe? Such an appeal was not made in vain. The dis-
comfitted Americans rally on the instant, and form into
line; the enemy halt, and dress their line; the American
Chief is between the adverse posts, as though he had been
placed there, a target for both. The arms of both lines
are leveled. Can escape from death be possible? Fitzgerald, horror-struck at the danger of his beloved commander, dropped the reins upon his horse's neck, and
drew his hat over his face, that he might not see him die.
A roar of musketry succeeds, and then a shout. It is the
shout of victory. The aid-de-camp ventures to raise his
eyes, and O glorious sight! the enemy are broken and
flying, while dimly amidst the glimpses of the smoke is
seen the Chief, alive, unharmed, waving his hat, and
cheering his comrades to the pursuit.

"Colonel Fitzgerald, celebrated as one of the finest
horsemen in the American army, now dashed his rowels
in his charger's flanks, and, heedless of the dead and
dying in his way, flew to the side of his Chief, exclaim-
ing, 'Thank God! your Excellency is safe!' The favorite

aid, a gallant and warm-hearted son of Erin, a man of thews and sinews, unused to the melting mood, now gave loose rein to his feelings, and wept like a child.

"Washington, ever calm amid scenes of the greatest excitement, affectionately grasped the hand of his aid and friend, and then ordered—'Away, my dear Colonel, and bring up the troops—the day is our own.'"

Washington was greatly distressed, during this period, by the introduction of the personal feelings of General Gates into his official relations with General Schuyler, and the resignation of the latter from the army, which, however, proved inacceptable even to the Congress, which contained so many friends of Gates. Schuyler's ability and integrity were so well known and so greatly valued that he was assured by Congress that further calumny should be silenced by the appointment of a committee to investigate fully all insinuations made against him. General Schuyler remained at his post in Albany while Gates proceeded to Congress, intent upon his own advancement.

The letter of James Duane, describing the conduct of Gates, is illuminating. He writes, "He was cheerfully admitted to the floor of the House, to make his communication by word of mouth. He took a seat in an elbow chair, and after telling us something about the Indians in the northern department, drew some papers from his pocket and commenced reading his complaints in an agitated voice and manner. He boasted of his patriotism in leaving his seat in Virginia for the hardships of camp life; and then, referring to what he was pleased to call his disgrace, his manner became violent, and he used many insulting words toward the Congress, and especially toward myself, whom he considered his enemy. I called him to order; and at the same time other members, offended by his unjust and offensive reproaches, also called him to order; and after a very warm debate, he was plainly informed that he could no longer be tolerated. His vanity leads him into many errors."

Apparently quite aside from any military operations against the enemy, Washington was frequently obliged to settle questions of rank and to eradicate petty jealousies from among his officers. The omission of Arnold's name from a list of promotions caused the Commander-in-chief to write to Richard Henry Lee, "A more active, a more spirited, and sensible officer, fills no department of your army. Not seeing him, then, in your list of major generals, and no mention made of him, has given me uneasiness; as it is not presumed, being the oldest brigadier, that he will continue in service under such a slight." To General John Sullivan he felt obliged to write a long letter concluding: "I shall quit it (the subject) with an earnest exhortation that you will not suffer yourself to be teased with evils that only exist in the imagination, and with slights that have no existence at all; keeping in mind, at the same time, that if distinct armies are to be formed, there are several gentlemen before you, in point of rank, who have a right to claim a preference."

Washington's opinion of Congress at this time is expressed in his reply to Robert Morris, of Philadelphia, who had responded nobly to appeals for money for the prosecution of the war, but who had wished for a more optimistic tone in the General's letters to Congress.

"To deceive Congress," replied Washington, "or you, through whose hands my letters to them are to pass, with false appearances and assurances, would in my judgment, be criminal, and make me responsible for the consequences. I endeavor, in all these letters, to state matters as they appear to my judgment, without adding or diminishing aught from the picture. From others my sentiments are hidden. . . . In a word, common prudence dictates the necessity of duly attending to the circumstances of both armies, before the style of conquerors is assumed by either; and sorry I am to add that this does not appear to be the case with us; nor is it in my power to make Congress fully sensible of the real situation of our affairs, and that it is with difficulty, if I may use the expression, that I can, by every means in my power, keep the life and soul of this army together. In a word, when they are at a distance, they think it is but to say, *presto, begone!* and everything is done. They seem not to have any conception of the difficulty and perplexity attending those who are to execute. Indeed, sir, your observations on the want of many capital characters in that senate are but too just. However, our cause is good, and I hope Providence will support it."

The evacuation of Ticonderoga was a blow keenly felt by Washington, but his unwavering sense of justice impelled him to write to Schuyler: "I will not condemn, or even pass a censure upon, any officer unheard, but I think it a duty which General St. Clair owes to his own character to insist upon an opportunity of giving the reasons for his sudden evacuation of a post which, but a few days before, he, by his own letters, thought tenable at least for a while. People at a distance are apt to form wrong conjectures; and if General St. Clair has good reasons for the step he has taken, I think the sooner he justifies himself the better. I have mentioned these matters because he may not know that his conduct is looked upon as very unaccountable by all ranks of people in this part of the country. If he is reprehensible, the public have an undoubted right to call for that justice which is due from an officer who betrays or gives up his post in an unwarrantable manner."

Washington transmitted St. Clair's report to Congress without comment, although he requested that Arnold be sent to aid Schuyler at Fort Edward. At the same time he wrote to Schuyler, "I need not enlarge upon the well-known activity, conduct, and bravery of General Arnold. The proof he has given of all three have gained him the confidence of the public and of the army, the eastern troops in particular."

Washington's consistent recognition of the worth of any man who had proved of value, and his fidelity to friends, civil or military, is one of the outstanding traits of his character manifested throughout his lifetime.

His instantaneous appraisal of young Lafayette and his marked fondness for him, as in the case of Alexander Hamilton,* is an evidence of the warmth of his friend-

---

* Hamilton, at the age of twenty, joined Washington's staff, and for four years served as the Commander's secretary and confidential aid.

ships, once formed. Washington's confidence in a man being once established, only the most flagrant misconduct could shake it. To rumor and detraction he invariably turned a deaf ear, requiring absolute proof of defection before withdrawing his confidence. Probably the romantic circumstances under which Lafayette made his way to America,* and his plea to serve as a volunteer without rank at his own expense, predisposed Washington in his favor. At any rate, Lafayette was admitted to the councils-of-war at a time when the Commander was in great doubt as to the enemy's intentions.

After much deliberation Washington decided to leave Philadelphia. He wrote to the president of Congress, on August 23, 1777, "Tomorrow morning the army will move again, and I think to march it through the city without halting. I am induced to do this from the opinion of several of my officers and many friends in Philadelphia, that it may have some influence on the minds of the disaffected there, and those who are dupes to their artifices and opinions."

Lafayette, in his *Memoirs,* thus describes the march: "Eleven thousand men but tolerably armed, and still worse clad, presented a singular spectacle; in this parti-colored and often naked state, the best dresses were hunting-shirts of brown linen. Their tactics were equally irregular. They were arranged without regard to size, excepting that the smallest men were in the front rank.

---

* At the age of nineteen the young Frenchman, inflamed by a reading of the Declaration of Independence, bought a vessel and, without knowledge of his family, who would have opposed the move, set sail for America.

With all this, they were good-looking soldiers, conducted by zealous officers."

It is said that the parade of the troops had, to some extent, the effect Washington desired, although the inhabitants of the countryside were greatly alarmed by the appearance, a little later, of General Howe's army. The battle of Brandywine had the result of causing Congress to adjourn to Lancaster, taking with them all their public documents. In Philadelphia hospitalities showered upon Howe by British loyalists caused the facetious remark of Franklin, "Howe has not taken Philadelphia so much as Philadelphia has taken Howe."

Although himself defeated at Brandywine, Washington improved the moment by writing to the president of Congress congratulating him on "the success of our arms to the northward, and if some accident does not put them out of their present train, I think we may count upon the total ruin of Burgoyne."

It appears that in the incidents "to the northward" centering about Bemis Heights and culminating in the surrender of Burgoyne, Gates put forth almost as much effort for personal supremacy as he did for his country's cause. Commissioned to supersede Schuyler, he reached headquarters soon after the battle of Bennington. Schuyler is said to have acquainted him with all his plans, and to have placed himself at Gates's disposal. Writing to Washington he said, "I shall go on doing my duty, and in endeavoring to deserve your esteem." To Congress he wrote, "I am sensible of the indignity of being ordered from the command of the army at the time when an engagement must soon take place."

Gates managed to offend, not only Daniel Morgan, but also Benedict Arnold, whom he deprived of command, but whom he could not restrain from action. It is said that Arnold's unauthorized leadership at Bemis Heights was a powerful factor in the success of the Americans, and Gates himself later designated Morgan's riflemen as "the corps the army of General Burgoyne are most afraid of," although it is said that he omitted Morgan's name from his account to Congress of the surrender of Burgoyne.

Even "Old Put," as General Putnam was affectionately called in the army, was not always as willing to coöperate with his Commander-in-chief as perfect patriotism demanded.

Washington, in an effort to meet Howe upon somewhat equal terms, had sent north for troops, which were at length grudgingly supplied by Gates. Encountering Putnam on their march southward to join Washington, a part of these troops were detained by him for purposes of his own. Alexander Hamilton, sent by Washington to hurry them on, felt obliged to write peremptorily to Putnam: "I now, sir, in the most explicit terms, by his Excellency's authority, give it as a positive order from him that all the Continental troops under your command be immediately marched to King's Ferry, there to cross the river, and hasten to reinforce the army under him."

Hamilton's censure of Putnam was severe, but Washington ignored the incident, since it was followed by obedience to his order.

It was at the battle of Germantown that Washington

again disregarded all personal danger to an extent alarming to his staff. According to Custis, it was "while exert-
ing himself to rally his broken columns, the exposure of
his person became so imminent that his officers, after
affectionately remonstrating with him in vain, seized
the bridle of his horse." Custis continues: "The retreat,
under all circumstances, was quite as favorable as could
be expected. The whole of the artillery was saved, and
as many of the wounded as could be removed. The ninth
Virginia regiment, under Colonel Matthews, having
penetrated so far as to be without support, after a desperate resistance surrendered its remnant of a hundred
men, including its gallant colonel, who had received
several bayonet wounds. The British pursued but two
or three miles, making prisoners of the worn-out soldiers,
who, after a night-march of fifteen miles, and an action
of three hours, were found exhausted and asleep in the
fields and along the roads.

"But the most happy and imposing influences upon
America and her cause, resulting from the battle of
Germantown, were experienced abroad. 'Eh, mon Dieu,'
exclaimed the Count de Vergennes, the French minister
of foreign affairs, to the American commissioners in
Paris, 'what is this you tell me, Messieurs; another
battle and the British grand army surprised in its camp
at Germantown, Sir William and his veterans routed and
flying for two hours, and a great victory only denied to
Washington by a tissue of accidents beyond all human
control. Ah, ah, these Americans are an elastic people.
Press them down today, they rise tomorrow. And then,
my dear sirs, these military wonders to be achieved by

an army raised within a single year, opposed to the skill, discipline, and experience of European troops commanded by generals grown gray in war. The brave Americans, they are worthy of the aid of France. They will succeed at last.'"

Whether or not the aid of France was won because of the elasticity of the Americans at Germantown, there seems to be no reason to doubt Custis's description of the bearing of Washington at Valley Forge:

"The winter of 1777 set in early, and with unusual severity. The military operations of both armies had ceased, when a detachment of the southern troops were seen plodding their weary way to winter quarters at the Valley Forge. The appearance of the horse-guard announced the approach of the Commander-in-chief. The officer commanding the detachment, choosing the most favorable ground, paraded his men to pay their General the honors of the passing salute. As Washington rode slowly up, he was observed to be eyeing very earnestly something that attracted his attention on the frozen surface of the road. Having returned the salute with that native grace, that dignified air and manner, that won the admiration of the soldiery of the old Revolutionary day, the Chief reined up his charger, and, ordering the commanding officer of the detachment to his side, addressed him as follows: 'How comes it, sir, that I have tracked the march of your troops by the blood-stains of their feet upon the frozen ground? Were there no shoes in the commissary's stores, that this sad spectacle is to be seen along the public highways?' The officer replied: 'Your Excellency may rest assured that this sight is as painful to my feelings as it can be to yours. But there is no remedy within our reach. When the shoes were issued, the different regiments were served in turn; it was our misfortune to be among the last to be served, and the stores became exhausted before we could obtain even the smallest supply.'

"The General was observed to be deeply affected by his officer's description of the soldiers' privations and sufferings. His compressed lips, the heaving of his manly chest, betokened the powerful emotions that were struggling in his bosom, when, turning toward the troops with a voice tremulous yet kindly, Washington exclaimed, *'Poor fellows!'* Then giving rein to his charger, he rode away.

"During this touching interview every eye was bent upon the Chief, every ear was attentive to catch his words; and when those words reached the soldiers, warm from the heart of their beloved commander, and in tones of sorrow and commiseration for their sufferings, a grateful, but subdued expression burst from every lip, of 'God bless your Excellency, your poor soldiers' friend.' "

The gloomy scene at Valley Forge was enlivened by the exchange for General Prescott, and the appearance in camp of Charles Lee. He had complained to Congress of his close confinement, although, by order of General Howe, he was quartered in a three-room suite in the New York City Hall, where he enjoyed the society of the British officers, and occupied himself with much correspondence, some of which was later found to be of a treasonable nature.*

---

* See page 184.

CHAPTER IX

CONSPIRACY AGAINST WASHINGTON

At the time when Washington's heart was wrung by the sufferings of his hungry, freezing soldiers, he was mortified and dismayed to learn that men in whom he had reposed confidence were insidiously working to undermine his reputation. As Lossing in his *Washington and the American Republic* has presented a comprehensive review of this loose conspiracy, his view of it is here quoted:

"General Conway appears to have been the most conspicuous man in this conspiracy, or at least the most incautious and public; and the affair is known in history as *Conway's Cabal.* Conway had come to America with the full expectation of receiving the commission of a major general in the Continental army. He was disappointed at the outset, but, hoping for speedy promotion, he joined the army under Washington. Boastful, intriguing, presumptuous, and selfish, he was purely a soldier of fortune. He sought only for personal advantages, and being utterly unprincipled in regard to the means by which his desires might be gratified, he greatly disgusted Washington, not only at the first interview, but throughout the campaign. Finally, when rumors reached the Chief that Conway was to be promoted to major general, over many worthier officers, he wrote a letter of remonstrance to Richard Henry Lee, in Congress, on the seventeenth of October, in which he said: 'In a word, the service is so difficult, and every necessary so expensive, that almost all our officers are tired out. Do not, therefore, afford them good pretexts for retiring. No day passes over my head without application for leave to resign. Within the last six days, I am certain, twenty commissions at least have been tendered to me. I must, therefore, conjure you to conjure Congress to consider this matter well, and not, by a real act of injustice, compel some good officers to leave the service, and thereby incur a train of evil unforeseen and irremediable. To sum up the whole, I have been a slave to the service; I have undergone more than most men are aware of, to harmonize so many discordant parts; but it will be impossible for me to be of any further service if such insuperable difficulties are thrown in my way. You may believe me, my good sir, that I have no earthly views but the public good in what I have said. I have no prejudice against General Conway, nor desire to serve any other brigadier, further than I think the cause will be benefited by it; to bring which to a speedy and happy conclusion is the most fervent wish of my soul.'

"This opposition to his schemes on the part of Washington, coming to the knowledge of Conway, filled him with indignation and malice, and made him a fit instrument to be employed against the Commander-in-chief.

"The chief leader of the opposition to Washington, in the army, appears to have been General Mifflin, who found in Conway, at this time, a ready helper in endeavors to disparage the military character of the Commander-in-chief, and elevate that of Gates; and in Congress the opposition was headed by James Lovell, a prominent member of the New England delegation. Toward the close of November Lovell wrote to Gates saying: 'You have saved our Northern Hemisphere, and in spite of consummate and repeated blundering, you have changed the condition of the southern campaign, on the part of the enemy, from offensive to defensive.' He then spoke of the prospect of the campaign closing, and of Washington's army going into winter-quarters, leaving the country exposed, thereby causing great dissatisfaction. 'So great,' he said, 'that nothing inferior to a proper commander-in-chief will be able to resist the mighty torrent of public clamor and public vengeance. We have a noble army melted down by ill-judged marches—marches that disgrace the authors and directors, and which have occasioned the severest and most just sarcasm and contempt of our enemies. How are you to be envied, my dear General! How different your conduct and your fortune!'

"Then, after speaking of a blind attempt 'to save a gone character,' Lovell remarks: 'Conway, Spottswood, Conner, Ross, and Mifflin have resigned, and many other good and brave officers are preparing their letters to Congress on the same subject. In short, this army will be totally lost unless you come down and collect the virtuous band who wish to fight under your banner, and with their aid save the Southern Hemisphere. Prepare yourself for a jaunt to this place—Congress must send for you.'

"These words of Lovell reveal the spirit of the whole matter, and it is needless to say that Gates entered into

the schemes with all his heart, for the long-coveted prize
for which he had aspired appeared to be in the custody
of these plotters against the Commander-in-chief.

"The first important movement in this conspiracy
was the sending of anonymous letters to the president
and several members of the Continental Congress, to
Patrick Henry, then governor of Virginia, and, it is
believed, to the presiding officers of several state legislatures, in which were abundant complaints, insinuations,
and exaggerated statements, and ascribing the misfortunes of the army to the incapacity or ill-timed policy of
the Commander-in-chief. A comparison between the
operations of the armies under the respective commands
of Washington and Gates was also drawn, with strong
coloring unfavorable to the former.

"A little later, the influence of the cabal in Congress
was plainly manifested, by the appointment of Conway
inspector general, and raising him to the rank of major
general, notwithstanding the strong language of Washington respecting his incapacity, and the danger that
might arise from his promotion.

"From time to time a little of the secret machinations of the cabal were brought to the notice of Washington, but with a nobility of soul which his traducers
had no conception by experience, he chose to suffer in
silence rather than injure the republican cause by a personal defense. 'My enemies,' he said, in a letter to the
president of Congress, when the matter became a subject
for correspondence, 'take an ungenerous advantage of me.
They know the delicacy of my situation, and that motives
of policy deprive me of the defense I might otherwise

make against their insidious attacks. They know I can not combat their insinuations, however injurious, without disclosing secrets which it is of the utmost moment to conceal.'

"And in a letter to his friend, Patrick Henry, who at once forwarded to Washington the anonymous letter he had received, the Chief, after assuring him that at no time since the landing of Howe at the Head of Elk had his army been equal in numbers to that of the enemy, and that the prevalence of tories in Pennsylvania prevented vigorous measures there, said: 'I have left to fight two battles, in order, if possible, to save Philadelphia, with less number than composed the army of my antagonist, whilst the world has given us at least double. This impression, though mortifying in some points of view, I have been obliged to encourage, because, next to being strong, it is best to be thought so by the enemy; and to this cause, principally, I think is to be attributed the slow movements of General Howe.

" 'How different the case in the northern department! There the states of New York and New England, resolving to crush Burgoyne, continued pouring in their troops till the surrender of that army; at which time not less than fourteen thousand militia, composed, for the most part, of the best yeomanry in the country, were well-armed, and in many instances supplied with provision of their own carrying. Had the same spirit pervaded the people of this and the neighboring states, we might, before this time, have had General Howe nearly in the situation of General Burgoyne, with this difference, that the former would never have been out of reach of his ships, whilst the latter increased his danger every step he took, having but one retreat in case of a disaster, and that blocked up by a respectable force!

" 'My own difficulties, in the course of the campaign, have not been a little increased by the extra aid of continental troops, which the gloomy prospect of our affairs in the North, immediately after the reduction of Ticonderoga, induced me to spare from this army. But it is to be hoped that all will yet end well. If the cause is advanced, indifferent is it to me where or in what quarter it happens.' The last sentence is a true reflex of the disinterested patriotism that filled the heart and governed the actions of the Commander-in-chief.

"Early in November the conspiracy was revealed to Washington in definite shape, through the officiousness of Colonel Wilkinson, who, as we have seen, was Gates's bearer of dispatches to the Congress concerning the surrender of Burgoyne. That body was then in session, in York, in Pennsylvania, and it was no less than eighteen days after that surrender before Wilkinson appeared upon the senate floor with the papers, and made his pompous announcement of the victory. After his arrival at York he employed three days in the preparation of his budget, and evidently expected to produce a great effect and receive a rich reward.

"But the Congress, mortified, no doubt, by the neglect of Gates to inform Washington of his victory, yet lacking courage to rebuke so grave an insult to the Commander-in-chief, were so tardy in making any award that Wilkinson, in his disappointment, and with an ill-concealed affectation of indifference, wrote to Gates, saying: 'I have not been honored with any mark of distinction from Congress. Indeed, should I receive no testimony of their approbation of my conduct, I shall not be mortified. My hearty contempt of the world will shield me from such pitiful sensation.' A just idea of the value of his services, so tardily rendered, was no doubt expressed by Samuel Adams, who, when it was proposed to vote Wilkinson a sword, gravely moved, instead, that 'the young gentleman should be presented with a pair of *spurs*.' A few days afterwards Wilkinson was breveted a brigadier general, and he appears to have been satisfied.

"On his way from the camp to the senate, Wilkinson stopped at Reading, where he spent an entire day with the lady whom he afterwards married. Lord Stirling* had his headquarters there, and with his military family Wilkinson appears to have had a free talk about things in general. He was doubtless acquainted with the schemes of the cabal, and desired to sound Lord Stirling respecting his opinion of the ability of Washington to perform the duties of his station. This, as a subordinate officer, he could do only through his own peer; so, in the course of conversation, he repeated to Major M'Williams, Stirling's aid-de-camp, a part of the contents of a letter which Gates had received from Conway, containing strictures on the management of the army under Washington, accompanied by reflections disparaging to the Chief. This was communicated to Lord Stirling, and he, as in duty bound, informed his Commander-in-chief of the extracts

* Lord Stirling was born in America but inherited his title. He served with distinction in the Continental army, and was one of Washington's most trusted officers.

from Conway's letter, as repeated by Wilkinson, with the remark that 'such wicked duplicity of conduct I shall always think it my duty to detect.'

"With his usual dignified forbearance, and governed by a nobility of sentiment that scorned to stoop even to reproach a man like Conway, Washington simply informed him, by the following note, that his treachery was known:

" 'Sir: A letter which I received last night contained the following paragraph: "In a letter from General Conway to General Gates, he says, Heaven has determined to save your country, or a weak general and bad counselors would have ruined it."

" 'I am, sir, your humble servant.

" 'George Washington.'

"This note conveyed a terrible rebuke. Had a blazing bombshell fallen at the feet of the leaders in the conspiracy, they could not have been more astounded than when this note was made known. Conway was dismayed, and hastened to Mifflin with the intelligence. That officer immediately wrote to Gates, saying: 'My dear General, an extract from Conway's letter to you has been procured and sent to headquarters. The extract was *a collection of just sentiments,* yet such as should not have been intrusted to any of your family. General Washington inclosed it to Conway without remark.' He then advised Gates to be more cautious. 'Take care of your sincerity and frank disposition,' he said; 'they can not injure yourself, but may injure some of your best friends. Affectionately yours,' etc.

"Gates was, at that time, the recipient of fulsome adulation from his admirers and friends, and lay dreaming, as it were, upon a bed of roses, of laurel wreaths for his brow, and a guaranty of immortality as the savior of the republic. Mifflin's letter broke the spell. It was like wormwood poured into the sweet drafts that were constantly pressed to his lips. Washington's note was terribly brief. How much or what had been communicated to the Chief, he knew not. Who is the traitor? was a question that greatly perplexed him. He did not suspect Wilkinson, his favorite, and fawning servant. He questioned the gentlemen of his staff, but all properly disavowed any knowledge of the matter. This increased his perplexity and perturbation of mind; but from a mean insinuation made by Wilkinson, he was led to suspect that Colonel Hamilton, during his late visit to his quarters, had received the information, and had been the channel of communication of it to his Chief.

"Assuming a tone of virtuous indignation, and the position of an injured man, Gates wrote to Washington, on the eighth of December, conjuring him to assist in tracing out 'the authors of the infidelity which put extracts from General Conway's letter' into the hands of his Commander-in-chief. 'Those letters,' he said, 'have been stealingly copied, but which of them, when, and by whom, is to me an unfathomable secret.' He thought his Excellency would do him, 'and the United States, a very important service,' he said, 'by detecting a wretch who may betray me, and capitally injure the very operations under your immediate directions. . . . It being unknown to me,' he continued, 'whether the letter came to you from a member of Congress, or from an officer, I shall have the honor of transmitting a copy of this to the president, that the Congress may, in concert with your Excellency, obtain as soon as possible a discovery which so deeply affects the safety of the states. Crimes of that magnitude may not remain unpunished.'

"Gates's chief object in sending a copy of his letter to the Congress was, doubtless, to inform his friends there of the treachery, and to put them on their guard. It did not reach Washington until the close of December, and on the fourth of January, the Commander-in-chief replied to it through the same channel, with characteristic candor and dignity. 'Your letter of the eighth ultimo,' he said, 'came to my hands a few days ago, and to my great surprise, informed me that a copy of it had been sent to Congress, for what reason I find myself unable to account; but as some end, doubtless, was intended to be answered by it, I am laid under the disagreeable necessity of returning my answer through the same channel, lest any member of that honorable body should harbor an unfavorable suspicion of my having practiced some indirect means to come at the contents of the confidential letters between you and General Conway.'

"He then informed Gates of the circumstance of Wilkinson's communication to Major M'Williams, and its transmission to headquarters. Then reciting the note to Conway, he remarked: 'Neither this letter, nor the information which occasioned it, was ever, directly or indirectly, communicated by me to a single officer in this army, out of my own family, excepting the Marquis de Lafayette, who, having been spoken to on the subject by

General Conway, applied for and saw, under injunctions of secrecy, the letter which contained Wilkinson's information; so desirous was I of concealing every matter that could, in its consequences, give the smallest interruption to the tranquillity of this army, or afford a gleam of hope to the enemy by dissension therein.

" 'Thus, sir, with an openness and candor which I hope will ever characterize and mark my conduct, have I complied with your request.

" 'The only concern I feel upon the occasion, finding how matters stand, is, that in doing this I have necessarily been obliged to name a gentleman, who, I am persuaded, although I never exchanged a word with him upon the subject, thought he was rather doing an act of justice, than committing an act of infidelity; and sure I am, that, till Lord Stirling's letter came to my hands, I never knew that General Conway, whom I viewed in the light of a stranger to you, was a correspondent of yours; much less did I suspect that I was the subject of your confidential letters. Pardon me, then, for adding that so far from conceiving that the safety of the states can be affected, or in the smallest degree injured by a discovery of this kind, or that I should be called upon in such solemn terms to point out the author, I considered the information as coming from yourself, and given with a friendly view to forewarn, and, consequently, to forearm me, against a secret enemy, or, in other words, a dangerous incendiary; in which character, sooner or later, this country will know General Conway. But in this, as in other matters, of late, I have found myself mistaken.'

"No language could have conveyed a more stinging

rebuke to Gates than this dignified letter. Hitherto, the whole matter had been a secret with a few, but now, the Congress having been made the medium of communication between the Commander-in-chief and Gates upon the subject of the conspiracy, it was blazoned to the world, and the mischievous cabal was subjected to the scorn of all honest and patriotic men.

"Washington's explanation, of course, caused a rupture between Gates and Wilkinson. The former, in a letter to Washington, charged Wilkinson with deceit and prevarication, and of meanly attempting to fix suspicion upon Colonel Troup, one of Gates's aids-de-camp. Gates also pronounced the pretended extract from Conway's letter 'a wicked and malicious forgery,' but he never fortified his assertion by producing the original, in which, 'if produced,' said Wilkinson, 'words to the same effect will appear.' In this assertion Wilkinson was finally sustained. The original letter, which was seen by President Laurens and others, contained not precisely those words, but in tenor the whole document was accurately represented by Wilkinson. Gates and Wilkinson said many hard things of each other, in connection with this affair, and, doubtless, both spoke the truth.

"Another phase of the factious movement was exhibited in the appointment of a new board of war, and in its operations. The organization took place on the twenty-seventh of November. Gates was placed at the head of the board, and Mifflin was one of its most active members. Another was Joseph Trumbull, the friend of Gates and the enemy of Schuyler; and the other two were Colonel Timothy Pickering (a New England officer), and Richard Peters, of Pennsylvania. The latter was a warm friend of Mifflin. The constitution of this board was an indication of the influence then at work in Congress, in favor of Gates and his friends.

"The president of Congress was instructed to communicate to Gates intelligence of his appointment, and to express the high sense of the important position in which he had been placed. He was also informed that he might officiate in the board or in the field, as occasion might require; and he was requested to repair to the Congress without delay, to enter upon his new duties.

"It was, doubtless, the intention of the cabal to make a strong and decisive movement toward the appointment of Gates as commander-in-chief, on his arrival. His warm friend, Lovell, wrote on the day of his appointment: 'We want you at different places, but we want you most near Germantown. Good God! What a situation we are in; how different from what might have been justly expected! You will be astonished when you know accurately what numbers have, at one time and another, been collected near Philadelphia, to wear out stockings, shoes, and breeches. Depend upon it, for every ten soldiers placed under the command of our Fabius, five recruits will be wanted, annually, during the war. . . . If it was not for the defeat of Burgoyne, and the strong appearance of a European war, our affairs are Fabiused into a very disagreeable posture.'

"Gates gladly accepted the office of president of the board of war, for it was invested with large powers, and, by delegated authority, was allowed to assume functions that belonged properly to the commander-in-chief. These

powers Gates at once put into requisition. Not doubting
that he would soon be made commander-in-chief, he
planned an expedition against Canada, hoping to enter
upon the duties of his exalted station with all the éclat
which a scheme of that kind would give. There was
another motive for this expedition very apparent. The
cabal wished to detach Lafayette from the person of
Washington, and enlist him in their interest, and for
that purpose the Marquis was appointed to the command
of the forces to go into Canada. This whole expedition
was planned by Gates, and the appointment of the leader
made without consulting Washington; and the first intimation that his Excellency had of the movement was
from Lafayette, who communicated a letter on the subject from the board of war.*

"Just at this moment Washington received further
information of the conspiracy to injure him. His lifelong
friend, Doctor Craik, wrote to him on the fourth of
January, saying: 'Base and villainous men, through
chagrin, envy, or ambition, are endeavoring to lessen
you in the minds of the people, and are taking underhand
methods to traduce your character. The morning I left
camp, I was informed by a gentleman whom I believe
to be a true friend of yours that a strong faction was
forming against you in the new board of war, and in
the Congress. It alarmed me exceedingly, and I wished
that he had informed me of it a day or two sooner, that
I might have taken an opportunity of mentioning it to
you. He begged that I would do it before I went away;
but upon consideration, I thought I had better defer it

* Gates later gave up his plan of moving against Canada, but
Lafayette never wavered in his loyalty to Washington.

until I reached home, as perhaps I might make some further discoveries on my way. At my arrival in Bethlehem I was told of it there, and was told that I should hear more of it on my way down. I did so, for at Lancaster I was still assured of it. All the way down I heard of it, and I believe it is pretty general over the country. No one would pretend to affix it on particulars, yet all seem to believe it.'

"Doctor Craik then referred to some of the members of the cabal, and to General Mifflin in particular. 'I have reason to believe,' he said, 'that he is not your friend, from many circumstances. The method they are taking is by holding General Gates up to the people, and making them believe that you have had a number three or four times greater than the enemy, and have done nothing; that Philadelphia was given up by your management, and that you have had many opportunities of defeating the enemy; and many other things as ungenerous and unjust. These are the low artifices they are making use of. It is said they dare not appear openly as your enemies, but that the new board of war is composed of such leading men as will throw such obstacles and difficulties in your way as to force you to resign. Had I not been assured of these things from such authority that I can not doubt them, I should not have troubled you with this. My attachment to your person is such, my friendship is so sincere, that every hint which has a tendency to hurt your honor wounds me most sensibly, and I write this that you may be apprized, and have an eye toward these men, and particularly General Mifflin. He is plausible, sensible, popular, and ambitious, takes great pains to draw over every officer he meets to his own way of thinking, and is very engaging.'

"Until the close of March, the subject under consideration was a topic for correspondence, in which Washington, Gates, Wilkinson, Patrick Henry, Doctor Gordon (the historian of the war), and anonymous writers, participated, some with words explanatory and some exculpatory. The attempt to elevate Gates upon the ruins of Washington's reputation was an utter failure, and all who participated in the scheme were soon heartily ashamed, and earnestly desired to put in disclaimers that might shield them from the odium which their conduct so richly entitled them to.

"General Gates, in a letter to a friend, dated at York, fourth of April, 1778, said: 'For my part, I solemnly declare I never was engaged in any plan or plot for the removal of General Washington, nor do I believe any such plot ever existed.' Mifflin also wrote, about that time: 'I never desired to have any person whomsoever take the command of the American Army from him (Washington), nor have I said or done anything of or respecting him which the public service did not require,' etc. Botta, after weighing the evidence against the designated leaders of the intrigue, draws therefrom the inevitable conclusion of their guilt, and says: 'The leaders of this combination, very little concerned for the public good, were immoderately so for their own, and the aim of all their efforts was to advance themselves and their friends at the expense of others.'

"The true character of General Conway, so early discovered by Washington, became, at length, well understood by the Congress. He was made to feel the scorn of the army officers because of his participation in the conspiracy against their beloved leader. This scorn, coupled with their personal dislike, made his position a very unpleasant one, and in an impertinent and complaining letter to the president of Congress, he intimated a wish to resign. A motion to accept his resignation was immediately carried. Conway was astonished and disappointed, and immediately repaired to York to ask to be restored. He said he did not wish to resign, and attempted explanations. It was too late. He could not longer be made a useful tool of intriguing men. The current of public opinion was against him, and he was cast aside. He went to Philadelphia, where he indulged in abusive language toward almost everybody. This deportment finally resulted in a duel between himself and General Cadwalader, on the fourth of July, 1778, in which Conway was severely wounded. His speedy death was expected, and under the impression that he could not long survive, he wrote the following note to Washington, as a reparation for the personal injuries he had inflicted:

" 'Sir: I find myself just able to hold the pen during a few minutes, and take this opportunity of expressing my sincere grief for having done, written, or said anything disagreeable to your Excellency. My career will soon be over; therefore, justice and truth prompt me to declare my last sentiments. You are, in my eyes, the great and good man. May you long enjoy the love, veneration, and esteem of these states, whose liberties you have asserted by your virtues. I am with the greatest respect, etc.'

"Conway recovered. Deprived of employment, deserted by his former friends, and everywhere despised by the people, he soon left the country.

"Washington, in a letter to Patrick Henry, at the close of March, gave his closing observations on the subject as follows: 'My caution to avoid anything which would injure the service prevented me from communicating, but to a very few of my friends, the intrigues of a faction which I knew was formed against me, since it might serve to publish our internal dissensions; but their own restless zeal to advance their views has too clearly betrayed them, and made concealment on my part fruitless. I can not precisely mark the extent of their views, but it appeared in general that General Gates was to be exalted on the ruin of my reputation and influence. This I am authorized to say, from undeniable fact in my possession, from publications, the evident scope of which would not be mistaken, and from private detractions industriously circulated. General Mifflin, it is commonly supposed, bore the second part in the cabal; and General Conway, I know, was a very active and malignant partisan; but I have good reasons to believe that their machinations have recoiled most sensibly upon themselves.' "

Never did the disinterested patriotism of Washington shine more clearly than in his magnanimous treatment of those who had so injured him. When the facts became known, Gates's popularity declined, though Washington, far from bringing any charges against him, continued to support him until the disaster at Camden indicated that his value to the service was doubtful.

CHAPTER X

WASHINGTON ENCOURAGED

The news that France had allied herself with the American cause was received at Valley Forge with great joy. An enthusiastic demonstration took place there, and evidences of encouragement reached Washington from all sides. Robert Morris wrote to him, "Most sincerely do I give you joy. Our independence is undoubtedly secured; our country must be free." Washington's remark to Putnam, "I hope the fair, and I may say, *certain* prospect of success, will not induce us to relax," is characteristic of his unfailing equipoise.

Perhaps as a result of the disclosures with regard to the Conway correspondence, all officers were required to take an oath of allegiance to the American cause. One notable hesitation, which caused much surprise, and considerable laughter, among the assembled officers, was that of Charles Lee. He is said to have complied, at last, with the remark, "As to King George, I am ready enough to absolve myself from all obligations to him, but I have some scruples about the Prince of Wales."

On the departure of the British from Philadelphia in the spring of 1778, Lee appeared to have a "superior knowledge" of the intentions of Sir Henry Clinton, and advised a mere following of the army, rather than the more aggressive policy which Washington advocated. The Commander-in-chief, however, on the advice of his

most trusted generals, decided to attack the British at
Monmouth Courthouse.

It is Custis who tells of the midnight visit of the Reverend David Griffith, chaplain and surgeon in the Virginia line, to Washington's tent on the night preceding
the battle. Washington, while his troops rested, was
hard at work upon plans for the proposed attack. Strict
orders had been given that he should not be disturbed,
but he made an exception in favor of the chaplain. Custis
states that Doctor Griffith unburdened himself of the
solemn warning: "While I am not permitted to divulge
the names of the authorities from whom I have obtained
my information, I can assure you they are of the very
first order, whether in point of character or attachment
to the cause of American independence. I have sought
this interview to warn your Excellency against the conduct of Major General Lee in tomorrow's battle."

The prediction proved all too true. For no apparent
reason, but to thwart the Commander-in-chief's plans,
Lee, instead of attacking, wasted some time in skirmishing, and then ordered a general retreat. The account
of Washington's rage on beholding Lee's troops, the
flower of the army, in headlong flight, has not been
exaggerated.

Custis states that during the heated conversation between Washington and Lee, "an incident of rare and
chivalric interest occurred. Lieutenant Colonel Hamilton, aid to the General-in-chief, leaped from his horse,
and, drawing his sword, addressed the General with,
'We are betrayed; your Excellency and the army are betrayed; and the moment has arrived when every true

friend of America and her cause must be ready to die in their defense.' Washington, charmed with the generous enthusiasm of his favorite aid, yet deemed the same ill-timed, and pointing to the colonel's horse that was cropping the herbage, unconscious of the great scene enacting around him, calmly observed, 'Colonel Hamilton, you will take your horse.' "

Custis relates other incidents of the day which he had doubtless heard many times over from the lips of participants in the battle:

"The General-in-chief now set himself in earnest about restoring the fortunes of the day. He ordered Colonel Stewart and Lieutenant Colonel Ramsey, with their regiments, to check the advance of the enemy, which service was gallantly performed; while the General, in person, proceeded to form his second line. He rode, on the morning of the twenty-eighth of June, and for that time only during the war, a white charger that had been presented to him. From the overpowering heat of the day, and the deep and sandy nature of the soil, the spirited horse sank under his rider, and expired on the spot. The Chief was instantly remounted upon a chestnut mare, with a flowing mane and tail, of Arabian breed, which his servant Billy was leading. It was upon this beautiful animal, covered with foam, that the American General flew along the line, cheering the soldiers in the familiar and endearing language ever used by the officer to the soldier of the Revolution, 'Stand fast, *my boys,* and receive your enemy; the southern troops are advancing to support you.'

"The person of Washington, always graceful, dignified, and commanding, showed to peculiar advantage when mounted; it exhibited, indeed, the very *beau ideal* of a perfect cavalier. The good Lafayette, during his last visit to America,* delighted to discourse of the 'times that tried men's souls.' From the venerated friend of our country we derived a most graphic description of Washington on the field of battle. Lafayette said, 'At Monmouth I commanded a division and, it may be supposed, I was pretty well occupied; still I took time, amid the roar and confusion of the conflict, to admire our beloved Chief, who, mounted on a splendid charger, rode along the ranks amid the shouts of the soldiers, cheering them by his voice and example, and restoring to our standard the fortunes of the fight. I thought then, as now,' continued Lafayette, 'that never had I beheld so *superb a man.'*

"Heedless of the remonstrances and entreaties of his officers, the Commander-in-chief exposed his person to every danger throughout the action of the twenty-eighth of June. The night before the battle of Monmouth a party of the general officers assembled, and resolved upon a memorial to the Chief, praying that he would not expose his person in the approaching conflict. His high and chivalric daring and contempt for danger at the battle of Princeton, and again at Germantown, where his officers seized the bridle of his horse, made his friends the more anxious for the preservation of a life so dear to all, and so truly important to the success of the common cause. It was determined that the memorial should be presented by Doctor Craik, the companion-in-arms of

* In 1824-1825.

Colonel Washington in the war of 1755; but Craik at once assured the memorialists that, while their petition would be received as a proof of their affectionate regard for their General's safety, it would not weigh a feather in preventing the exposure of his person, should the day go against them, and the presence of the Chief become important at the post of danger. Doctor Craik then related the romantic and imposing incident of the old Indian's prophecy, as it occurred on the banks of the Ohio in 1770, observing that, bred, as he himself was, in the rigid discipline of the Kirk of Scotland, he possessed as little superstition as anyone, but that really there was a something in the air and manner of an old savage chief delivering his oracle amid the depths of the forest that time or circumstance would never erase from his memory, and that he believed, with the tawny prophet of the wilderness, that their beloved Washington was the spirit-protected being described by the savage, that the enemy could not kill him, and that while he lived, the glorious cause of American Independence would never die.

"On the following day, while the Commander-in-chief, attended by his officers, was reconnoitering the enemy from an elevated part of the field, a round-shot from the British artillery struck but a little way from his horse's feet, throwing up the earth over his person, and then bounding harmlessly away. The Baron Steuben, shrugging up his shoulders, exclaimed, 'Dat wash very near,' while Doctor Craik, pleased with this confirmation of his faith in the Indian's prophecy, nodded to the officers who composed the party of the preceding evening, and then, pointing to Heaven, seemed to say, in the words of the savage prophet, 'The Great Spirit protects him; he can not die in battle.'

"A ludicrous occurrence varied the incidents of the twenty-eighth of June. The servants of the general officers were usually well-armed and mounted. Will Lee, or Billy, the former huntsman and favorite body-servant of the Chief, a square, muscular figure, and capital horseman, paraded a corps of valets, and riding pompously at their head, proceeded to an eminence crowned by a large sycamore tree, from whence could be seen an extensive portion of the field of battle. Here Billy halted and, having unslung the large telescope that he always carried in a leathern case, with a martial air applied it to his eye, and reconnoitered the enemy. Washington, having observed these maneuvers of the corps of valets, pointed them out to his officers, observing, 'See those fellows collecting on yonder height? The enemy will fire on them to a certainty.' Meanwhile the British were not unmindful of the assemblage on the height, and perceiving a burly figure well-mounted, and with a telescope in hand, they determined to pay their respects to the group. A shot from a six-pounder passed through the tree, cutting away the limbs, and producing a scampering among the corps of valets, that caused even the grave countenance of the General-in-chief to relax into a smile.

"Nor must we omit, among our incidents of the battle of Monmouth, to mention the achievement of the famed Captain Molly, a *nom de guerre* given to the wife of a matross in Proctor's artillery. At one of the guns of Proctor's battery six men had been killed or wounded. It was deemed an unlucky gun, and murmurs arose that it should be drawn back and abandoned. At this juncture, while Captain Molly was serving some water for the refreshment of the men, her husband received a shot in the head, and fell lifeless under the wheels of the piece. The heroine threw down the pail of water, and crying to her dead consort, 'Lie there, my darling, while I avenge ye,' grasped the ramrod that the lifeless hand of the poor fellow had just relinquished, sent home the charge, and called to the matrosses to prime and fire. It was done. Then entering the sponge into the smoking muzzle of the cannon, the heroine performed the duties of the expert artilleryman while loud shouts from the soldiers rang along the line. The doomed gun was no longer deemed unlucky, and the fire of the battery became more vivid than ever. The Amazonian fair one kept to her post till night closed the action, when she was introduced to General Greene, who, complimenting her upon her courage and conduct, the next morning presented her to the Commander-in-chief. Washington received her graciously, gave her a piece of gold, and assured her that her services should not be forgotten.

"On the night of the memorable conflict Washington lay down in his cloak under a tree, in the midst of his brave soldiers. About midnight an officer approached cautiously, fearful of awakening him, when the Chief called out, 'Advance, sir, and deliver your errand. I lie here *to think and not to sleep.*'

"In the morning the American army prepared to renew the conflict, but the enemy had retired during the night, leaving their dead and many wounded to the care of the victors. Morgan's mountaineers pursued on their trail and made some captures, particularly the coach of a general officer.

"The British grand army embarked for Staten Island. The number, order, and regularity of the boats, and the splendid appearance of the troops, rendered this embarkation one of the most brilliant and imposing spectacles of the Revolutionary War.

"Congress passed a unanimous vote of thanks to the General-in-chief, his officers, and soldiers for the promptness of their march from Valley Forge, and their surprise and defeat of the enemy; and a *feu de joie* was fired by the whole American army for the victory of Monmouth."

The rebuke which Washington administered to Lee, in the presence of officers and soldiers, caused that volatile warrior to write to his superior officer, "I think, sir, I have a right to demand some reparation for the injury committed; and unless I can obtain it, I must, in justice to myself, when this campaign is closed, which I believe will close the war, retire from the service at the head of which is placed a man capable of offering such injuries."

To this Washington replied, "As soon as circumstances will permit, you shall have an opportunity of justifying yourself to the army, to Congress, to America, and to the world in general, or of convincing them that you were guilty of a breach of orders, and of misbehavior before the enemy on the twenty-eighth instant, in not attacking them as you had been directed, and in making an unnecessary, disorderly, and shameful retreat."

Upon Lee's expressing a desire for a court-martial, Washington sent him, by an officer delegated to place him under arrest, a copy of the charges on which he was to be tried. The charges are quoted:

"First: Disobedience of orders in not attacking the enemy on the twenty-eighth of June, agreeable to repeated instructions.

"Secondly: Misbehavior before the enemy on the same day, by making an unnecessary, disorderly, and shameful retreat.

"Thirdly: Disrespect to the Commander-in-chief, in two letters, dated the first of July and the twenty-eighth of June."

During the course of the court-martial, which held sessions at various places in the progress of the army, Lee wrote to his friend, Colonel Joseph Reed, a naïve and probably sincere comment upon the character of Washington, "No attack, it seems, can be made on General Washington but it must recoil on the assailant." He added: "I never entertained the most distant wish or intention of attacking General Washington. I have ever honored and respected him as a man and as a citizen; but, if the circle which surrounds him choose to erect him into an infallible divinity, I shall certainly prove a heretic; and if, great as he is, he can be persuaded to attempt wounding everything I ought to hold dear, he must thank his priests if his deityship gets scratched in the scuffle."

Lee was found guilty of all charges, though the word "shameful" was omitted. He was suspended from the army for one year, this verdict being confirmed by the vote of Congress.

Thereafter Washington avoided all mention of Lee

except in official communications, although Lee published many newspaper articles in which Washington and other officers were unfavorably presented. Lee's reinstatement in the army was prevented largely by an impudent letter he wrote to Congress.

It was not until the close of 1857 that the "Plan of Mr. Lee, 1777," was discovered among some papers offered for sale in New York. This manuscript "Plan" came into the possession of Professor George H. Moore, librarian of the New York Historical Society, who immediately recognized its significance. It is in Lee's handwriting, covering eight pages of foolscap, dated the twenty-ninth of March, 1777, in which he outlined to Sir William Howe a plan for the conquest of the colonies. Evidently this is a part of the writing with which he whiled away the days of his captivity when not entertaining officers of the British army. It solves the puzzling doubts entertained by his contemporaries.

That Washington could excuse a breach of discipline, and even flagrant disobedience of orders, is indicated by his leniency to Daniel Morgan on the one occasion of the latter's departure from the most perfect rectitude. The incident is narrated by Custis. Although he does not state the time exactly, it was probably in the period of uncertainty which preceded the battle at Monmouth. Custis tells that he had "the honor and happiness of an interview with the old general, which lasted for several days," and proceeds, "General Morgan related to us the substance of the following personal reminiscences; and many times during the recital his voice faltered with emotion, and his eyes filled with tears.

"The outposts of the two armies were very near to each other, when the American Commander, desirous of obtaining particular information respecting the positions of his adversary, summoned the famed leader of the riflemen, Colonel Daniel Morgan, to headquarters.

"It was night, and the Chief was alone. After his usual polite, yet reserved and dignified, salutation, Washington remarked: 'I have sent for you, Colonel Morgan, to entrust to your courage and sagacity a small but very important enterprise. I wish you to reconnoiter the enemy's lines, with a view to your ascertaining correctly the positions of their newly-constructed redoubts; also of the encampments of the British troops that have lately arrived, and those of the Hessian auxiliaries. Select, sir, an officer, non-commissioned officer, and about twenty picked men, and under cover of the night proceed with all possible caution, get as near as you can, learn all you can, and by day-dawn retire and make your report to headquarters. But mark me, Colonel Morgan, mark me well: On no account whatever are you to bring on any skirmishing with the enemy. If discovered, make a speedy retreat; let nothing induce you to fire a single shot. I repeat, sir, that no force of circumstances will excuse the discharge of a single rifle on your part, and for the extreme preciseness of these orders, permit me to say that I have my reasons.' Filling two glasses of wine, the General continued, 'And now, Colonel Morgan, we will drink a good-night, and success to your enterprise.' Morgan quaffed the wine, smacked his lips, and assuring his Excellency that his orders should be punctually obeyed, left the tent of the Commander-in-chief.

"Charmed at being chosen the executive officer of a daring enterprise, the Leader of the Woodsmen repaired to his quarters, and calling for Gabriel Long, his favorite captain, ordered him to detail a trusty sergeant and twenty prime fellows. When these were mustered, and ordered to lay on their arms, to be ready at a moment's warning, Morgan and Long stretched their manly forms before the watchfire, to await the going down of the moon—the signal for departure.

"A little after midnight, and while the rays of the setting moon still faintly glimmered in the western horizon, 'Sergeant,' cried Long, 'stir up your men!' And twenty athletic figures were upon their feet in a moment. Indian file, march, and away all sprang with the quick, yet light and stealthy, step of the woodsmen. They reached the enemy's lines, crawled up so close to the pickets of the Hessians as to inhale the odor of their pipes, and discovered, by the newly turned-up earth, the position of the redoubts, and the encampment of the British and German reinforcements. In short, they performed their perilous duty without the slightest discovery; and, pleased with themselves, and the success of their enterprise, prepared to retire.

"The adventurous party reached a small eminence at some distance from the British camp and commanding an extensive prospect over the adjoining country. Here Morgan halted, to give his men a little rest, before taking up his line of march for the American outposts. Scarcely had they thrown themselves on the grass when they perceived, issuing from the enemy's advanced pickets, a body of horse, commanded by an officer, and proceeding along a road that led directly by the spot where the riflemen had halted. No spot could be better chosen for an ambuscade, for there were rocks and ravines, and also scrubby oaks, that grew thickly on the eminence by which the road we have just mentioned passed, at not exceeding a hundred yards.

"'Down boys, down!' cried Morgan, as the horse approached. 'Lie close there, my lads, till we see what these fellows are about!'

"Meantime the horsemen had gained the height and, the officer dropping his rein on his charger's neck, with a spy-glass reconnoitered the American lines.

"Morgan looked at Long, and Long upon his superior, while the riflemen, with panting chests and sparkling eyes, were only awaiting some signal from their officers 'to let the ruin fly.'

"At length the martial ardor of Morgan overcame his prudence and sense of military subordination. Forgetful of consequences, reckless of everything but his enemy now within his grasp, he waved his hand, and loud and sharp rang the report of the rifles amid the surrounding echoes.

"At point-blank distance the certain and deadly aim of the Hunting Shirts of the Revolutionary army is too well known to history to need remark. The effects of the fire of the riflemen were tremendous. Of the horsemen, some had fallen to rise no more; others, wounded, but entangled in their stirrups, were dragged by the furious animals, while the very few who were unscathed spurred hard to regain the shelter of the British lines.

"While the smoke yet canopied the scene of slaughter, and the picturesque forms of the woodsmen appeared among the foliage, as they were reloading their pieces, the colossal figure of Morgan stood apart. The martial shout with which he was wont to cheer his comrades in the hour of combat was hushed; the shell from which he had blown full many a note of battle and of triumph on the fields of Saratoga hung idly by his side; no order was given to spoil the slain. The arms and equipments for which there was always a bounty from Congress, the shirts for which there was much need in that, the sorest period of our country's privations—all, all, were abandoned, as, with an abstracted air and a voice struggling for utterance, Morgan suddenly turning to his captain, exclaimed, 'Long, to the camp! march!' The favorite captain obeyed; the riflemen, with trailed arms, fell into file; and Long and his party soon disappeared, but not before the hardy fellows had exchanged opinions on the strange termination of the late affair.

"Morgan followed slowly on the trail of his men. The full force of his military guilt had rushed upon his mind, even before the reports of his rifles had ceased to echo in the neighboring forests. He became more and more convinced of the enormity of his offense, as he soliloquized:

" 'Well, Daniel Morgan, you have done for yourself. Broke, sir, broke to a certainty. You may go home, sir, to the plow; your sword will be of no further use to you. Broke, sir, nothing can save you; and there is the end of Colonel Morgan. Fool, fool—by a single act of madness thus to destroy the earnings of so many toils, and many a hard-fought battle. You are broke, sir, and there is an end of Colonel Morgan.'

"There suddenly appeared, at full speed, the aid-de-camp, who, reining up, accosted the colonel with, 'I am ordered, Colonel Morgan, to ascertain whether the firing just now heard, proceeded from your detachment.' 'It did, sir,' replied Morgan, doggedly. 'Then, Colonel, continued the aid, 'I am further ordered to require your immediate attendance upon his Excellency.' Morgan bowed, and the aid, wheeling his charger, galloped back to rejoin his Chief.

"The gleams of the morning sun upon the saber of the horse-guard announced the arrival of the dreaded commander. With a stern, yet dignified, composure Washington addressed the military culprit: 'Can it be possible, Colonel Morgan, that my aid-de-camp has informed me aright? Can it be possible, after the orders you received last evening, that the firing we have heard proceeded from your detachment? Surely, sir, my orders were so explicit as not to be easily misunderstood.' Morgan was brave, but it has been often and justly, too, observed, that that man never was born of woman who could approach the great Washington and not feel a degree of awe and veneration from his presence. Morgan quailed for a moment before the stern yet just displeasure of his Chief, till, arousing all his energies to the effort, he uncovered, and replied, 'Your Excellency's orders were perfectly well understood; and, agreeably to the same, I proceeded with a select party to reconnoiter the enemy's lines by night. We succeeded even beyond our expectations, and I was returning to headquarters to make my report when, having halted a few minutes to rest the men, we discovered a party of horse coming out from the enemy's lines.

They came up immediately to the spot where we lay concealed by the brushwood. There they halted and, gathered up together like a flock of partridges, affording me so tempting an opportunity of annoying my enemy, that—that—may it please your Excellency—flesh and blood could not refrain.'

"At this rough, yet frank, bold, and manly explanation, a smile was observed to pass over the countenances of several of the General's suite. The Chief remained unmoved; when, waving his hand, he continued: 'Colonel Morgan, you will retire to your quarters, there to await further orders.' Morgan bowed, and the military *cortège* rode on to the inspection of the outposts.

"Arrived at his quarters, Morgan threw himself upon his hard couch, and gave himself up to reflections upon the events which had so lately and so rapidly succeeded each other. The hours dragged gloomily away. Night came, but with it no rest for the troubled spirit of poor Morgan. The drums and fifes merrily sounded the soldiers' dawn, and the sun arose, giving 'promise of a good day.'

"About ten o'clock the orderly on duty reported the arrival of an officer of the staff from headquarters, and Lieutenant Colonel (Alexander) Hamilton, the favorite aid of the Commander, entered the marquee. 'Be seated,' said Morgan; 'I know your errand; so be short, my dear fellow, and put me out of my misery at once. I know that I am arrested; 'tis a matter of course. Well, there is my sword; but surely his Excellency honors me, indeed, in these, the last moments of my military existence, when he sends for my sword by his favorite aid, and my most esteemed friend. Ah, my dear Hamilton, if you knew what I have suffered since the cursed horse came out to tempt me to my ruin.'

"Hamilton, about whose strikingly-intelligent countenance there always lurked a playful smile, now observed, 'Colonel Morgan, his Excellency has ordered me to'——'I know it,' interrupted Morgan, 'to bid me prepare for trial. But pshaw, why a trial! Guilty, sir, guilty past all doubt. But then (recollecting himself), perhaps my services might plead—nonsense! against the disobedience of a positive order. No, no, it is all over with me, Hamilton! There is an end of your old friend, and of Colonel Morgan.' The agonized spirit of our hero then mounted to a pitch of enthusiasm as he exclaimed, 'But my country will remember my services, and the British and Hessians will remember me too, for though I may be far away, my brave comrades will do their duty, and Morgan's riflemen be, as they always have been, a terror to the enemy.'

"The noble, the generous-souled, Hamilton could no longer bear to witness the struggle of the brave unfortunate. 'My orders,' he said, 'are to invite you to dine with his Excellency today at three o'clock precisely; yes, my brave and good friend, Colonel Morgan, you still are, and are likely long to be, the valued and famed commander of the rifle regiment.'

"Morgan sprang from the camp-bed on which he was sitting and, seizing the hand of the little great man in his giant grasp, wrung and wrung, till the aid-de-camp literally struggled to get free, then exclaimed, 'Am I in my senses! But I know you, Hamilton; you are too noble a

fellow to sport with the feelings of an old brother-soldier.'
Hamilton assured his friend that all was true, and gayly
kissing his hand as he mounted his horse, and bidding
the now delighted colonel to remember three o'clock
and be careful not to disobey a second time, he galloped
to the headquarters.

"Morgan entered the pavilion of the Commander-in-
chief, as it was fast filling with officers, all of whom, after
paying their respects to the General, filed off to give a
cordial squeeze of the hand to the commander of the rifle
regiment, and to whisper in his ear words of congratula-
tion. The cloth removed, Washington bade his guests
fill their glasses, and gave his unvarying toast, *'All our
Friends.'* Then, with his usual old-fashioned politeness,
he drank to each guest by name. When he came to
'Colonel Morgan, your good health, sir,' a thrill ran
through the manly frame of the gratified and again
favorite soldier, while every eye in the pavilion was
turned upon him. At an early hour the company broke
up, and Morgan had a perfect escort of officers accompanying him to his quarters, all anxious to congratulate
him upon his happy restoration to rank and favor, all
pleased to assure him of their esteem for his person and
services.

"And often in his after life did Morgan reason upon
the events which we have transmitted to the Americans
and their posterity, and he would say: 'What could the
unusual clemency of the Commander-in-chief toward so
insubordinate a soldier as I was, mean? Was it that my
attacking my enemy wherever I could find him, and the
attack being crowned with success, should plead in bar

of the disobedience of a positive order? Certainly not. Was it that Washington well knew I loved, nay adored, him above all human beings? That knowledge would not have weighed a feather in the scale of his military justice. In short, the whole affair is explained in five words: *It was my first offense.'*

"The clemency of Washington toward the *first offense* preserved to the army of the Revolution one of its most valued and effective soldiers, and had its reward in little more than two years from the date of our narrative, when Brigadier General Morgan established his own fame and shed an undying luster on the arms of his country, by the glorious and ever-memorable victory of the Cowpens."

CHAPTER XI

EXERTIONS UNABATED

The echoes of Lee's defection had hardly ceased when Washington was called upon to soothe the wounded feelings of Count D'Estaing, the commander of the French fleet,* in consequence of a tactless expression of opinion by General Sullivan, in command of the Rhode Island troops. In concert with the American generals D'Estaing had planned a combined land and naval attack on Newport. But before the attack could take place, D'Estaing learned that an English fleet was approaching. At once he put to sea to engage it in battle. Again his plans were frustrated, when a sudden storm shattered his fleet, and necessitated his sailing to Boston for repairs.

On the eleventh of September, 1778, Washington wrote to the French commander as follows. Although he was keenly disappointed by the unfavorable turn of events, the Commander allowed no hint of any such feeling to appear in his letter to the Count.

"If the deepest regret that the best-concerted enterprise and bravest exertions should have been rendered fruitless by a disaster, which human prudence was incapable of foreseeing or preventing, can alleviate disappointment, you may be assured that the whole continent sympathizes with you. It will be a consolation to you to reflect that the thinking part of mankind do

* Sent, in 1778, to aid the United States.

not form their judgment from events; and that their equity will ever attach equal glory to those actions which deserve success, and those which have been crowned with it. It is in the trying circumstances to which your Excellency has been exposed that the virtues of a great mind are displayed in their brightest luster, and that a general's character is better known than in the moment of victory. It was yours, by every title that can give it; and the adverse elements, which robbed you of your prize, can never deprive you of the glory due to you. Though your success has not been equal to your expectations, yet you have the satisfaction of reflecting that you have rendered essential services to the common cause."

After a long review, in the letter, of the whole situation, Washington expressed his regret that harmony had been disturbed.

Throughout the war Washington was obliged to struggle with Congress and local executive bodies to obtain the necessities for his troops. Early in the year 1779 he wrote to the legislature of New Jersey: "For a fortnight past the troops, both officers and men, have been almost perishing for want. They have been alternately without bread or meat the whole time, with a very scanty allowance of either, and frequently destitute of both. Yet they have borne their sufferings with a patience that merits the approbation, and ought to excite the sympathies, of their countrymen." It is gratifying to learn that on this occasion the response of New Jersey was immediate and generous, though Congress continued to be reluctant to co-operate fully in supplying the needs of the army.

This reluctance may have been influenced by occasional instances of abuse of power, as in the case of General Benedict Arnold, who had been appointed military governor of Philadelphia in June, 1778, when the British evacuated the city. Arnold had married beautiful Margaret Shippen, and lived in great state, entertaining lavishly. The debts, which were the inevitable consequence of his extravagance, tempted him to make an unwarranted use of his official power.

It is said that he forbade the local merchants to sell certain staple commodities, and dealt in them himself, through agents, with great profits. This was an abuse of power which could not be tolerated, and the charges which were made against Arnold were referred to Washington by Congress for investigation.

After long delay a court-martial found Arnold guilty of two of the four charges made against him, and sentenced him to be reprimanded by the Commander.

Washington's invariable generosity toward offenders emanates from every line of his written rebuke: "Our profession is the chastest of all. Even the shadow of a fault tarnishes the luster of our finest achievements. The least inadvertence may rob us of public favor, so hard to be acquired. I reprimand you for having forgotten that, in proportion as you had rendered yourself formidable to your enemies, you should have been guarded and temperate in your deportment toward your fellow-citizens. Exhibit anew those noble qualities which have placed you on the list of our most valued commanders. I will furnish you, as far as it may be in my power, with opportunities of regaining the esteem of your country."

Arnold's wounded pride, coupled with enforced limitation to lawful sources of income, caused him to seek revenge as well as financial security at the expense of his country.

Americans are familiar with the details of his attempt to surrender the fortifications and garrison at West Point to Sir Henry Clinton, for the sum of fifty thousand dollars in gold and the commission of a brigadier general in the British Army.

Washington's own narration of Arnold's attempted betrayal of his country has come to us from the pen of Colonel Tobias Lear, private secretary to Washington and a resident in his home for a number of years. Writing in his diary, Lear made the following notes while the account was fresh in his memory:

"Mr. Drayton and Mr. Izard (gentlemen from South Carolina) here all day. After dinner General Washington was, in the course of conversation, led to speak of Arnold's treachery, when he gave the following account of it, which I shall put in his own words, thus: 'I confess I had a good opinion of Arnold before his treachery was brought to light; had that not been the case, I should have had some reason to suspect him sooner, for when he commanded in Philadelphia, the Marquis Lafayette brought accounts from France of the armament which was to be sent to co-operate with us in the ensuing campaign.

"'Soon after this was known, Arnold pretended to have some private business to transact in Connecticut, and on his way there he called at my quarters; and in the course of conversation expressed a desire of quitting

Philadelphia and joining the army for the ensuing campaign. I told him that it was probable we should have a
very active one, and that if his wound and state of health
would permit, I should be extremely glad of his services
with the army. He replied that he did not think his
wound would permit him to take a very active part; but
still he persisted in his desire of being with the army.
He went on to Connecticut, and on his return called
again upon me. He renewed his request of being with
me next campaign, and I made him the same answer I
had done before. He again repeated that he did not
think his wound would permit him to do active duty,
and intimated a desire to have the command at West
Point. I told him I did not think that would suit him, as
I should leave none in the garrison but invalids, because
it would be entirely covered by the main army. The
subject was dropped at that time, and he returned to Philadelphia. It then appeared somewhat strange to me that a
man of Arnold's known activity and enterprise should
be desirous of taking so inactive a part.

" 'When the French troops arrived at Rhode Island,
I had intelligence from New York that General Clinton
intended to make an attack upon them before they could
get themselves settled and fortified. In consequence of
that, I was determined to attack New York, which would
be left much exposed by his drawing off the British
troops; and accordingly formed my line of battle and
moved down with the whole army to King's Ferry,
which we passed.

" 'Arnold came to camp at that time, and having no
command, and consequently no quarters (all the houses

thereabouts being occupied by the army), he was obliged to seek lodgings at some distance from the camp. While the army was crossing at King's Ferry, I was going to see the last detachment over, and met Arnold, who asked me if I had thought of anything for him. I told him that he was to have the command of the light troops, which was a post of honor, and which his rank indeed entitled him to. Upon this information his countenance changed, and he appeared to be quite fallen; and instead of thanking me, or expressing any pleasure at the appointment, never opened his mouth. I desired him to go on to my quarters and get something to refresh himself, and I would meet him there soon. He did so.

" 'Upon his arrival there, he found Colonel Tilghman, whom he took a-one side, and mentioning what I had told him, seemed to express great uneasiness at it—as his leg, he said, would not permit him to be long on horseback; and intimated a great desire to have the command at West Point. When I returned to my quarters, Colonel Tilghman informed me of what had passed. I made no reply to it—but his behavior struck me as strange and unaccountable.

" 'In the course of that night, however, I received information from New York that General Clinton had altered his plan and was debarking his troops. This information obliged me likewise to alter my disposition and return to my former station, where I could better cover the country. I then determined to comply with Arnold's desire, and accordingly gave him the command of the garrison at West Point.

" 'Things remained in this situation about a fortnight,

when I wrote to the Count Rochambeau desiring to meet him at some intermediate place (as we could neither of us be long enough from our respective commands to visit the other), in order to lay the plan for the siege of Yorktown, and proposed Hartford, where I accordingly went and met the Count. On my return I met the Chevalier Luzerne, toward evening, within about fifteen miles of West Point (on his way to join the Count at Rhode Island), which I intended to reach that night, but he insisted upon turning back with me to the next public house; where, in politeness to him, I could not but stay all night, determining, however, to get to West Point to breakfast very early. I sent off my baggage, and desired Colonel Hamilton to go forward and inform General Arnold that I would breakfast with him.

" 'Soon after he arrived at Arnold's quarters, a letter was delivered to Arnold which threw him into the greatest confusion. He told Colonel Hamilton that something required his immediate attendance at the garrison which was on the opposite side of the river to his quarters; and immediately ordered a horse, to take him to the river; and the barge, which he kept to cross, to be ready; and desired Major Franks, his aid, to inform me, when I should arrive, that he was gone over the river and would return immediately.

" 'When I got to his quarters and did not find him there, I desired Major Franks to order me some breakfast; and as I intended to visit the fortifications, I would see General Arnold there. After I had breakfasted, I went over the river and, inquiring for Arnold, the commanding officer told me that he had not been there. I likewise inquired at the several redoubts, but no one could give me any information where he was. The impropriety of his conduct when he knew I was to be there struck me very forcibly, and my mind misgave me; but I had not the least idea of the real cause.

" 'When I returned to Arnold's quarters about two hours after, and told Colonel Hamilton that I had not seen him, he gave me a packet which had just arrived for me from Colonel Jameson, which immediately brought the matter to light.

" 'I ordered Colonel Hamilton to mount his horse and proceed with the greatest dispatch to a post on the river about eight miles below, in order to stop the barge if she had not passed; but it was too late.

" 'It seems that the letter Arnold received which threw him in such confusion was from Colonel Jameson, informing him that André was taken and that the papers found upon him were in his possession.

" 'Colonel Jameson, when André was taken with these papers, could not believe that Arnold was a traitor, but rather thought it was an imposition of the British in order to destroy our confidence in Arnold. He, however, immediately on their being taken, dispatched an express after me, ordering him to ride night and day till he came up with me. The express went the lower road, which was the road by which I had gone to Connecticut, expecting that I would return by the same route and that he would meet me; but before he had proceeded far, he was informed that I was returning by the upper road.

He then cut across the country and followed in my track till I arrived at West Point. He arrived about two hours after, and brought the above packet.

" 'When Arnold got down to the barge, he ordered his men, who were very clever fellows and some of the better sort of soldiery, to proceed immediately on board the "Vulture" sloop of war, as a flag, which was lying down the river; saying that they must be very expeditious, as he must return in a short time to meet me, and promised them two gallons of rum if they would exert themselves.

" 'They did accordingly; but when they got on board the "Vulture," instead of their two gallons of rum, he ordered the coxwain to be called down into the cabin and informed him that he and the men must consider themselves as prisoners. The coxwain was very much astonished, and told him that they came on board under the sanction of a flag. He answered that that was nothing to the purpose; they were prisoners.

" 'But the Captain of the "Vulture" had more generosity than this pitiful scoundrel, and told the coxwain that he would take his parole for going on shore to get clothes, and whatever else was wanted for himself and his companions. He accordingly came, got his clothes, and returned on board.

" 'When they got to New York, General Clinton, ashamed of so low and mean an action, set them all at liberty.' "

It was characteristic of Washington to refrain from expressing his feelings and convictions concerning those who had injured him. This dispassionate account of Arnold's treachery is a remarkable instance of that trait. We are told that in the midst of the intensive efforts to capture Arnold and to secure the stronghold of West Point against surprise, Washington paused to send word to Mrs. Arnold that her husband was "safe within the enemy's lines."

The unfortunate André was given the benefit of every possible leniency and kindness. After his trial and conviction by a court of fourteen officers of the American army, among them Greene, Lafayette, Steuben, and Knox, he was allowed to write freely to Sir Henry Clinton as well as to his family and friends. His execution was delayed one day to allow a committee appointed by Sir Henry to present additional evidence. No exculpatory evidence being presented, the execution was carried out.

Arnold's defection was a severe blow to the American cause, but as difficulties only seemed to arouse Washington to greater and more effective exertions, there was no immediate advantage to the British from Arnold's treason. It served to unify the patriots. Although momentarily shaken by many rumors against others which resulted in secret investigations, Washington's confidence in his generals was fully justified.

Among these the name of Nathanael Greene is preeminent. Custis confirms this belief in his remarks upon the favorites of Washington. "It has often been asked," he says, " 'Who were the favorites of Washington? Whom did he love?' I answer, the most worthy. . . . Yet such was his delicacy in bestowing praise, even where most deserved, that he declined the mentioning of Greene's division which had so gallantly covered the retreat from

Brandywine, saying to that illustrious commander, who prayed that his comrades might receive their well-earned commendation: 'You, sir, are considered in this army as my favorite officer; your division is composed of south-rons, my more intimate countrymen. Such are my reasons.'

"If I am asked," continues Custis, " 'And did not Washington unbend and admit to familiarity and social friendship some one person, to whom age and long and interesting association gave peculiar privilege, the privilege of the heart?' I answer, that favored individual was Robert Morris. The General-in-chief of the armies of independence, in the relief afforded the privations of his suffering soldiery, first learned the value of Robert Morris. It was he who brought order out of chaos and whose talent and credit sustained the cause of his country in her worst time."

CHAPTER XII

YORKTOWN

The beginning of the year 1781 marked the culmination of the suffering of the American soldier in the Revolution. General Anthony Wayne's record of their deprivations is eloquent. They were, he writes, "poorly clothed, badly fed, and worse paid, some of them not having received a paper dollar for nearly twelve months; exposed to winter's piercing cold, to drifting snow, and chilling blasts, with no protection but old worn-out coats, tattered linen overalls, and but one blanket between three men.

"The officers in general, as well as myself, find it necessary to stand for hours every day, exposed to wind and weather, among these poor naked fellows, while they are working at their huts and redoubts, often assisting with our own hands, in order to procure a conviction to their minds that we share, and more than share, every vicissitude in common with them; sometimes asking to participate in their bread and water. The good effect of this conduct is very conspicuous, and prevents their murmuring in public; but the delicate mind and eye of humanity are hurt, very much hurt, at their visible distress and private murmurings."

It was not until some of Wayne's troops mutinied in Pennsylvania that Congress and the people in general were aroused to act in their behalf. After a long period

A handwritten expense account ledger.

FACSIMILE OF A PART OF WASHINGTON'S EXPENSE ACCOUNT WITH THE UNITED STATES of enforced inactivity, Washington secured from France the loan which armed him to take the offensive. Marshaling all his forces with the greatest forethought, and securing the co-operation of the French with the most delicate tact, he struck the crippling blow for which he had so long and so patiently prepared. For its description we turn to Custis, whose *Memoirs* never fail to reveal some personal trait of that complex personality.

"The campaign of 1781 was considerably advanced, without any decided advantages to the combined armies, when the Chevalier de Barras, the commander of the French naval forces at Rhode Island, announced to General Washington that the Count de Grasse* would sail from the West Indies with a powerful fleet and three thousand troops, on the third of August, and might be expected in the Chesapeake about the first of September. Upon the receipt of this agreeable intelligence the allies lost no time in preparing for the investiture of New York; the Americans approaching gradually toward the city, and the French from Newport, the two armies forming a junction at Dobbs Ferry, on the Hudson. Large bodies of troops were moved toward Staten Island, the first object of attack; extensive magazines were collected, ovens built, and everything indicating that the fleet alone was wanting to commence the siege in earnest, when, in the midst of these demonstrations, the combined armies suddenly decamped, and masking New York, proceeded in full march for the south.

"The reasons that induced Washington thus to change the scene of his operations were, some of them, governed

---

* The French admiral placed in command of the new fleet sent to America in 1781.

by circumstances beyond his control, especially as regarded the co-operation of the French naval forces. The
Count de Grasse preferred the Chesapeake to the Bay
of New York, as being better suited to his large vessels,
while the admiral, being limited in his remaining in the
American waters to a certain and an early day, could
most conveniently render his assistance in the south.
This, together with other and imposing considerations,
induced the American general, while continuing to
threaten Sir Henry Clinton, to strike at Cornwallis in
Virginia.

"Sir Henry Clinton, aware that a powerful French
fleet was destined for the American coast, and presuming
that, upon its arrival, a combined attack would be made
upon New York, ordered Earl Cornwallis, then pursuing
his victorious career in Virginia, to fall down upon the
tidewater, and, after selecting a spot where he could conveniently embark a part of his troops to reinforce his
commander-in-chief, to entrench the remainder, and
await further orders. But the sudden and unexpected
march of the combined armies to the South entirely
changed the aspects of military affairs. It was now the
Earl, and not Sir Henry, that required reinforcement, and
Sir Henry again writing to his lordship, bade him
strengthen his position at Yorktown, promising him the
immediate aid of both land and naval forces.

"Meantime, Washington had written a letter to the
Marquis de Lafayette, then in Virginia, which he caused
to be intercepted. In the letter he remarked that he was
pleased with the probability that Earl Cornwallis would

fortify either Portsmouth or Old Point Comfort, *for, were he to fix upon Yorktown,* from its great capabilities of defense, he might remain there snugly and unharmed, until a superior British fleet would relieve him with strong reinforcements, or embark him altogether.

"This fated letter quieted the apprehensions of the British commander-in-chief as to the danger of his lieutenant, and produced those delays in the operations of Sir Henry that tended materially to the success of the allies and the surrender of Yorktown.

"The fleet of the Count de Grasse, consisting of twenty-eight sail-of-the-line, and a due proportion of frigates, containing three thousand veteran troops under the Marquis de St. Simon, anchored in the Chesapeake on the thirtieth of August. The frigates were immediately employed in conveying the troops up the James River, where they were landed and reinforced the army of Lafayette, who then commanded in Virginia. An instance of virtue and magnanimity that occurred at this period of our narrative adorns the fame and memory of Lafayette.

"Upon the arrival of the French land and naval forces in our waters, their commanders said to Lafayette: 'Now, Marquis, now is your time; a wreath of never-fading laurel is within your grasp! Fame bids you seize it. With the veteran regiments of St. Simon, and your own continentals, you have five thousand; to these add a thousand marines and a thousand seamen, to be landed from the fleet, making seven thousand good soldiers, which with your militia, give you an aggregate exceeding ten thousand men. With these, storm the enemy's works while they are yet in an unfinished state, and before the arrival of the combined armies you will end the war, and acquire an immortal renown.'

" 'Believe me, my dear sir,' said the good Lafayette, during his visit in America, 'this was a most tempting proposal to a young general of twenty-four, and who was not unambitious of fame by honest means; but insuperable reasons forbade me from listening to the proposal for a single moment. Our beloved General had intrusted to me a command far above my deserts, my age, or experience in war. From the time of my first landing in America, up to the campaign of 1781, I had enjoyed the attachment, nay, parental regards, of the matchless Chief. Could I then dare to attempt to pluck a leaf from the laurel that was soon to bind his honored brow—the well-earned reward of long years of toils, anxieties, and battles? And lastly, could I have been assured of success in my attack, from the known courage and discipline of the foe, that success must have been attended by a vast effusion of human blood.'

"The Commander-in-chief, accompanied by the Count de Rochambeau, arrived at Williamsburg, the headquarters of Lafayette, on the fourteenth of September. The General, attended by a numerous suite of American and French officers, repaired to Hampton, and thence on board the *Ville de Paris,* the French admiral's ship, lying at anchor in the chops of the capes, to pay their respects to the Count de Grasse, and consult with him as to their future operations.

"On the American Chief's reaching the quarter-deck, the admiral flew to embrace him, imprinting the French salute upon each cheek. Hugging him in his arms, he exclaimed, *'My dear little general!'* De Grasse was of lofty stature; but the term *petit,* or small, when applied to the majestic and commanding person of Washington, produced an effect upon the risible faculties of all present not to be described. The Frenchmen, governed by the rigid etiquette of the *ancien régime,* controlled their mirth as best they could; but our own jolly Knox, heedless of all rules, laughed, and that aloud till his fat sides shook.

"Washington returned from this conference by no means satisfied with its result. The admiral was extremely restless at anchor while his enemy's fleet kept the sea; and having orders limiting his stay in the American waters to a certain and that not distant day, he was desirous of putting to sea to block up the enemy's fleet in the basin of New York, rather than to run the risk of being himself blockaded in the bay of the Chesapeake.

"Washington urged De Grasse to remain, because his departure, he said, 'by affording an opening for the succor of York, which the enemy would instantly avail themselves of, would frustrate our brilliant prospects, and the consequence would be, not only the disgrace and loss of renouncing an enterprise, upon which the fairest expectations of the allies have been founded, after the most expensive preparations, but perhaps disbanding the whole army for want of provision.'

"Washington now dispatched Lafayette on a secret

mission to the Count; and never, in the whole course of
the Revolutionary contest, were the services of that friend
of America of more value to her cause than in the present instance.

"That all-commanding influence of Lafayette at this
period, not only with the French court, of which he was
the idol, but with the whole people of France; his powerful family connections with the high *noblesse,* particularly the distinguished family of De Noailles; all these
considerations enabled Lafayette to throw himself as a
shield between the Count de Grasse and any blame that
might be attached to him at home for yielding to the
views and wishes of the American Chief.

"The Marquis prevailed, and he soon returned to
headquarters with the gratifying intelligence that the
admiral had consented to remain at his anchors (unless
a British fleet should appear off the capes), and would
send a part of his vessels higher up the Bay, the better to
complete the investiture of Yorktown.

"On the fifth of September Admiral Graves, with
nineteen sail-of-the-line, appeared off the capes of Virginia. Count de Grasse immediately slipped his cables
and put to sea with twenty-four line-of-battle ships. An
engagement ensued, without material results to either
side, and, after four days of maneuvering, the French
fleet returned to its former anchorage, the British bearing away for New York.

"Meantime the Chevalier de Barras had arrived, with
eight sail-of-the-line, bringing a battering-train, and an
ample supply of all the munitions necessary for the siege.
These were speedily landed up the James River, and

many delays and disappointments occurred in their transportation to the lines before Yorktown, a distance of six
miles. Long trains of the small oxen of the country
tugged at a single gun, and it was not until the arrival
of the better teams of the grand army that much progress
could be made.

"The combined armies, arriving at the Head of Elk
(now Elkton), embarked a portion of the troops in transports; another portion were embarked at Baltimore;
while the remainder pursued the route by land to Virginia—the whole meeting at Williamsburg.

"On the twenty-eighth of September the allies moved
in four columns, in order of battle, and, the outposts of
the enemy being driven in, the first parallel was commenced. The work continued with such diligence that
the batteries opened on the night of the ninth of October, and a tremendous fire of shot and shell continued
without interruption. A red-hot shot from the French,
who were on the left, fell upon the "Gaudalope" and
"Charon," two British frigates. The latter, of forty-four
guns, was consumed, together with three transports.

"The defenses of the town were hourly sinking under
the effects of the cannonade from the American and
French batteries, when, on the night of the fourteenth,
it was determined to carry the two British redoubts on
the south, by the bayonet. For this service detachments
were detailed from both the American and French armies
—the former under the command of Lieutenant Colonel
Hamilton, long the favorite aid of the Commander-in-
chief, but now restored to his rank and duty in the line,
and the latter under the Baron de Viomenil.

"At a given signal the detachments advanced to the assault. As the Americans were mounting the redoubt, Lieutenant Colonel Laurens, aid-de-camp, appeared suddenly on their flank, at the head of two companies. Upon Major Fish hailing him with, 'Why, Laurens, what brought you here?' the hero replied, 'I had nothing to do at headquarters, so came here to see what you all were about.' Bravest among the brave, this Bayard of his age and country rushed with the foremost into the works, making, with his own hand, Major Campbell, the British commandant, a prisoner-of-war. The cry of the Americans as they mounted to the assault was, 'Remember New London!'*

"Washington, during the whole of the siege, continued to expose himself to every danger. It was in vain his officers remonstrated. It was in vain that Colonel Cobb, his aid-de-camp, entreated him to come down from a parapet, whence he was reconnoitering the enemy's works, the shot and shell flying thickly around, and an officer of the New England line killed within a very few yards. During one of his visits to the main battery a soldier of Colonel Lamb's artillery had his leg shattered by the explosion of a shell. As they were bearing him to the rear, he recognized the Chief, and cried out, 'God bless your Excellency; save me if you can, for I have been a good soldier, and served under you during the whole war.' Sensibly affected by the brave fellow's appeal, the General immediately ordered him to the particular

---

* In September, 1781, a large British force, under Benedict Arnold, had attacked New London (Connecticut), killed a number of its inhabitants, and practically laid the city in ashes.

care of Doctor Craik. It was too late; death terminated his sufferings after an amputation was performed.

"At this period of the siege occurred that sublime instance of patriotism when Governor Nelson directed the heavy shot and bomb-shells of the Americans to be cast upon his own fine house, in order to dislodge British officers who had their quarters there."

Lafayette's version of the incident, narrated years later, is well worth quoting:

"I had just finished a battery mounted with heavy pieces," said Lafayette, "but before I opened on the town, I requested the attendance of the Governor of Virginia, not only as a compliment due to the chief magistrate of the state in which I was serving, but from his accurate knowledge of the localities of a place in which he had spent the greater part of his life. 'To what particular spot would your Excellency direct that we should point the cannon?' I asked. 'There,' promptly replied the noble-minded, patriotic Nelson, 'to that house; it is mine, and is, now that the secretary's is nearly knocked to pieces, the best one in the town; and there you will be almost certain to find Lord Cornwallis and the British headquarters. Fire upon it, my dear Marquis, and never spare a particle of my property so long as it affords a comfort or a shelter to the enemies of my country.' The governor then rode away, leaving us all charmed with an instance of devotional patriotism that would have shed a luster upon the purest ages of Grecian or Roman virtue."

When the governor's house was fired upon, "Lord Cornwallis," writes Custis, "removed his headquarters to apartments excavated in the bank on the southern extremity of the town, where two rooms were wainscoted with boards, and lined with baize, for his accommodation. It was in that cavernous abode that the Earl received his last letter from Sir Henry Clinton. It was brought by the honorable Colonel Cochran, who, landing from an English cutter on Cape Charles, procured an open boat, and threading his way, under cover of a fog, through the French fleet, arrived safely, and delivered his dispatches. They contained orders for the Earl to hold out to the last extremity, assuring him that a force of seven thousand men would be immediately embarked for his relief.

"While taking wine with his lordship after dinner, the gallant colonel proposed that he should go up to the ramparts and take a look at the Yankees, and upon his return give Washington's health in a bumper. He was dissuaded from so rash a proceeding by everyone at the table, the whole of the works being at that time in so ruinous a state that shelter could be had nowhere. The colonel, however, persisted, and gayly observing that he would leave his glass as his representative till his return, which would be quickly, away he went. Poor fellow, he did return, and that quickly, but he was borne in the arms of the soldiers, not to his glass, but his grave.

"For a great distance around Yorktown the earth trembled under the cannonade, while many an anxious and midnight watcher ascended to the housetops to listen to the sound, and to look upon the horizon, lighted up by the blaze of the batteries, the explosions of the shells, and the flames from the burning vessels in the harbor.

"At length, on the morning of the seventeenth, the thundering ceased, hour after hour passed away, and the most attentive ear could not catch another sound. What had happened? Can Cornwallis have escaped? To suppose he had fallen was almost too much to hope for.

"After a fruitless attempt to escape, in which the elements, as at Long Island, were on the side of America and her cause, on the morning of the seventeenth Cornwallis beat a parley. Terms were arranged, and, on the nineteenth (of October, 1781), the British army laid down its arms.

"The imposing ceremony took place at two o'clock. The American troops were drawn up on the right, and the French on the left, of the high road leading to Hampton. A vast crowd of persons from the adjoining country attended to witness the ceremony.

"The captive army, in perfect order, marched in stern and solemn silence between the lines. All eyes were turned toward the head of the advancing column. Cornwallis, the renowned, the dreaded Cornwallis, was the object that thousands longed to behold. He did not appear, but sent his sword by General O'Hara, with an apology for his non-appearance on account of indisposition. It was remarked that the British soldiers looked only toward the French army on the left, whose appearance was assuredly more brilliant than that of the Americans, though the latter were respectable in both their clothing and appointments, while their admirable discipline and the hardy and veteran appearance of both officers and men showed they were no carpet knights, but soldiers who had seen service and were inured to war. Lafayette, at the head of his division, observing that the captives confined their admiration exclusively to the French army, neglecting his darling light-infantry, the very apple of his eye and pride of his heart, determined to bring 'eyes to the right.' He ordered his music to strike up Yankee Doodle. 'Then,' said the good general, 'they did look at us, my dear sir, but were not very well pleased.'

"When ordered to ground arms, the Hessian was content. He was tired of the war; his pipe and his patience pretty well exhausted, he longed to bid adieu to toilsome marches, battles, and the heat of the climate that consumed him. Not so the British soldier; many threw their arms to the ground in sullen despair. One fine veteran fellow displayed a soldierly feeling that excited the admiration of all around. He hugged his musket to his bosom, gazed tenderly on it, pressed it to his lips, then threw it from him, and marched away in tears.

"On the day of the surrender the Commander-in-chief rode his favorite and splendid charger, named Nelson, a light sorrel, sixteen hands high, with white face and legs. This famous charger died at Mount Vernon many years after the Revolution, at a very advanced age. After the Chief had ceased to mount him, he was never ridden, but grazed in a paddock in summer, and was well cared for in winter; and as often as the retired farmer of Mount Vernon would be making a tour of his grounds, he would halt at the paddock, when the old war-horse would run, neighing, to the fence, proud to be caressed by the master's hands.

"The day after the surrender Earl Cornwallis repaired to headquarters to pay his respects to General Washington and await his orders. The captive chief was received with all the courtesy due to a gallant and unfortunate foe. The elegant manners, together with the manly, frank, and soldierly bearing of Cornwallis, soon made him a prime favorite at headquarters, and he often formed part of the suite of the Commander-in-chief in his rides to inspect the leveling of the works previous to the retirement of the combined armies from before Yorktown.

"At the grand dinner given at the headquarters to the officers of the three armies, Washington filled his glass, and, after his invariable toast, whether in peace or war, of *'All our Friends,'* gave *'The British Army,'* with some complimentary remarks upon its chief, his proud career in arms, and his gallant defense of Yorktown. When it came to Cornwallis's turn, he prefaced his toast by saying that the war was virtually at an end, and the contending parties would soon embrace as friends; there might be affairs of posts, but nothing on a more enlarged scale, as it was scarcely to be expected that the ministry would send another army to America. Then turning to Washington, his lordship continued: 'And when the illustrious part that your Excellency has borne in this long and arduous contest becomes matter of history, fame will gather your brightest laurels rather from the banks of the Delaware than from those of the Chesapeake.' In this his lordship alluded to the memorable midnight march made by Washington with the shattered remains of the grand army, aided by the Pennsylvania militia, on the night of the second of January, 1777, which resulted in the surprise of the enemy in his rear, and the victory of Princeton, restoring hope to the American cause when it was almost sinking in despair.

"Colonel Tarleton, alone of all the British officers of rank, was left out in the invitations to headquarters. Gallant and high-spirited, the colonel applied to the Marquis de Lafayette to know whether the neglect might not have been accidental. Lafayette well knew that accident had nothing to do with the matter, but referred the applicant to Lieutenant Colonel Laurens, who, as aid-de-camp to the Commander-in-chief, must, of course, be able to give the requisite explanation. Laurens at once said, 'No, Colonel Tarleton, no accident at all; intentional, I can assure you, and meant as a reproof for certain cruelties practiced by the troops under your command in the campaigns of the Carolinas.'—'What, sir,' haughtily rejoined Tarleton, 'and is it for severities inseparable from war, which you are pleased to term cruelties, that I am to be disgraced before junior officers? Is it, sir, for a faithful discharge of my duty to my king and my country, that I am thus humiliated in the eyes of three armies?' —'Pardon me,' continued Colonel Laurens, 'there are modes, sir, of discharging a soldier's duty, and where mercy has a share in the mode, it renders the duty the more acceptable to both friends and foes.' Tarleton stalked gloomily away to his quarters, which he seldom left until his departure from Virginia.

"The weather during the siege of Yorktown was propitious in the extreme, being, with the exception of the squall on the night of the sixteenth, the fine autumnal

weather of the South, commonly called the Indian summer, which greatly facilitated the military operations.
Washington's headquarters were under canvas the whole
time.

"A domestic affliction threw a shade over Washington's happiness while his camp still rang with shouts of
triumph for the surrender of Yorktown. His step-son
(John Parke Custis), to whom he had been a parent and
protector, and to whom he was fondly attached, who had
accompanied him to the camp at Cambridge, and was
among the first of his aids in the dawn of the Revolution,
sickened while on duty as extra aid to the Commander-
in-chief in the trenches before Yorktown. Aware that
his disease (the camp-fever) would be mortal, the sufferer had yet one last lingering wish to be gratified, and
he would die content. It was to behold the surrender of
the sword of Cornwallis. He was supported to the
ground, and witnessed the admired spectacle, and was
then removed to Eltham, a distance of thirty miles from
camp.

"An express from Dr. Craik announced that there was
no longer hope, when Washington, attended by a single
officer and a groom, left the headquarters at midnight
and rode with all speed to Eltham.

"The anxious watchers by the couch of the dying
were, in the gray of twilight, aroused by a trampling of
horse, and, looking out, discovered the Commander-in-
chief alighting from a jaded charger in the courtyard. He
immediately summoned Doctor Craik, and to the eager
inquiry, 'Is there any hope?' Craik mournfully shook his
head. The General retired to a room to indulge his grief,

requesting to be left alone. In a little while the poor
sufferer expired. Washington, tenderly embracing the be-
reaved wife and mother, observed to the weeping group
around the remains of him he so dearly loved, 'From this
moment I adopt his two youngest children as my own.'
Absorbed in grief, he then waved with his hand a melancholy adieu, and, fresh horses being ready, without rest
or refreshment, he remounted and returned to the camp."

The two children thus adopted by Washington were
Eleanor Parke Custis, aged two and a half years, and
George Washington Parke Custis, infant-in-arms, later
the author of the *Memoirs,* from which this account of
the siege of Yorktown is quoted.

CHAPTER XIII

CONSTRUCTIVE STATESMANSHIP

Washington, after the burial of John Parke Custis, made a hurried trip to Mount Vernon, pausing only at Fredericksburg to visit his mother. The son of John Parke Custis, in his *Memoirs,* gives a hint of the feeling which prevailed. "In the village of Fredericksburg all was joy and revelry; the town was crowded with the officers of the French and American armies, and with gentlemen for many miles around, who hastened to welcome the conquerors of Cornwallis. The citizens got up a splendid ball, to which the matron (Mary Washington) was invited. She observed that although her dancing days were pretty well over, she should feel happy in contributing to the general festivity, and consented to attend.

"The foreign officers were anxious to see the mother of their Chief. They had heard indistinct rumors touching her remarkable life and character, but forming their judgments from European examples, they were prepared to expect in the mother that glitter and show which would have been attached to the parents of the great in the countries of the old world. How were they surprised when, leaning on the arm of her son, she entered the room, dressed in the very plain, yet becoming, garb worn by the Virginia lady of the old time. Her address, always dignified and imposing, was courteous, though reserved. She received the complimentary attentions which were paid to her without evincing the slightest elation, and at an early hour, wishing the company much enjoyment of their pleasures, observed that it was high time for old folks to be in bed, and retired, leaning as before on the arm of her son.

"The foreign officers were amazed in beholding one whom so many causes conspired to elevate, preserving the even tenor of her life, while such a blaze of glory shone upon her name and offspring. It was a moral spectacle such as the European world had furnished no examples. Names of ancient lore were heard to escape from their lips; and they declared, 'if such are the matrons in America, well may she boast of illustrious sons.'"

Arrived at Mount Vernon, Washington wrote to General Greene, expressing a sense of deep anxiety for the welfare of his country, which had not been allayed by his military success. "I shall remain but a few days here," he wrote, "and shall proceed to Philadelphia, where I shall attempt to stimulate Congress to the best improvement of our late success, by taking the most vigorous and effectual measures to be ready for an early and decisive campaign the next year. My greatest fear is that Congress, viewing this stroke in too important a point of light, may think our work too nearly closed, and will fall into a state of languor and relaxation. To prevent this error I will employ every means in my power, and if unhappily we sink into that fatal mistake, no part of the blame shall be mine."

Arrived at Philadelphia, the Commander wrote to

Greene again: "I am apprehensive that the states, elated by the late success, and taking it for granted that Great Britain will no longer support so losing a contest, will relax in their preparations for the next campaign. I am detained here by Congress to assist in the arrangements for the next year; and I shall not fail, in conjunction with the financier, the minister of foreign affairs, and the secretary of war, who are all most heartily well-disposed, to impress upon Congress, and get them to impress upon the respective states, the necessity of the most vigorous exertions."

Philadelphia welcomed Washington with great honor, and even Congress now found it impossible to deny the requests of the victor. It was indeed a propitious moment for Benjamin Franklin, in France, to secure from the French government a loan of six million dollars.

Meanwhile the French fleet sailed from the Chesapeake, although the French troops under Rochambeau remained in Virginia. Lafayette, anxious to visit his family, obtained leave of absence for that purpose from Congress. The American army was stationed on the Hudson and in the Jerseys, to be ready to besiege New York in the spring, and a force under St. Clair was dispatched to the south.

Washington, although informed by Sir Guy Carleton that Admiral Digby and he had been appointed joint commissioners to arrange a truce or peace, did not relax his vigilance.

It was at about this time that he received a letter from an officer in the American army which aroused his indignation. Colonel Lewis Nicola of Pennsylvania may have expressed the wishes of many veterans. He presented to Washington an argument for the formation of a government similar to that of England, saying: "In this case, it will, I believe, be uncontroverted that the same abilities which have led us through difficulties apparently unsurmountable by human power to victory and glory—those qualities that have merited and obtained the universal esteem and veneration of an army—would be most likely to conduct and direct us in the smoother paths of peace. Some people have so connected the ideas of tyranny and monarchy as to find it very difficult to separate them. It may, therefore, be requisite to give the head of such a constitution as I propose some title apparently more moderate; but, if all other things were once adjusted, I believe strong arguments might be produced for admitting the title of *king,* which I conceive would be attended with some national advantage."

Washington, while sympathizing with the sufferings of the army which may have inspired this proposal, refused to entertain a thought of it. Personal aggrandizement had no part in his efforts for the welfare of his country. His patriotism was pure and disinterested. He replied to Nicola in terms which forever prohibited further suggestions of that nature.

"With a mixture of great surprise and astonishment," he wrote, "I have read with attention the sentiments you have submitted to my perusal. Be assured, sir, no occurrence in the course of this war has given me more painful sensations than your information of there being such ideas existing in the army as you have expressed, and which I must view with abhorence and reprehend with severity. For the present, the communication of them will rest in my own bosom, unless some further agitation of the matter shall make a disclosure necessary. I am much at a loss to conceive what part of my conduct could have given encouragement to an address which to me seems big with the greatest mischiefs that can befall my country. If I am not deceived in the knowledge of myself, you could not have found a person to whom your schemes are more disagreeable. At the same time, in justice to my own feelings, I must add that no man possesses a more serious wish to see ample justice done to the army than I do; and, as far as my power and influence, in a constitutional way, extend, they shall be employed to the utmost of my abilities to effect it, should there be any occasion. Let me conjure you, then, if you have any regard for your country, concern for yourself or posterity, or respect for me, to banish these thoughts from your mind, and never communicate, as from yourself or any one else, a sentiment of the like nature."

During the tedious negotiations for peace, there was much unrest in the army. It was while reading an address to a group of disaffected veterans that a personal appeal of Washington was seen to carry more weight with them than all the abstract reasoning which he brought to bear. After reading the first paragraph of his address, he laid down his manuscript in order to put on his spectacles. His simple remark, "You see I have grown gray in your service, and am now growing blind," touched every heart, bringing tears to the eyes of veterans whose own vision he felt had become blinded in another sense by the hardships of war.

In the groping of the bewildered states for an effective form of government Washington sent a circular letter to the governor of each state, saying: "There are four things which I humbly conceive are essential to the well-being, I may even venture to say, to the existence of the United States, as an independent power.

"First: An indissoluble union of the states under one federal head.

"Secondly: A sacred regard to public justice.

"Thirdly: The adoption of a proper peace establishment, and,

"Fourthly: The prevalence of that pacific and friendly disposition among the people of the United States which will induce them to forget their local prejudices and politics, to make those mutual concessions which are requisite to the general prosperity, and in some instances to sacrifice their individual advantages to the interest of the community."

The final treaty of peace having been signed on September 3, 1783, the Continental army was disbanded. The Americans having taken possession of the posts vacated by the British, Washington was about to go to Annapolis to surrender his commission to Congress. He met his officers in the parlor of Fraunce's Tavern to take leave of them. At the moment of bidding farewell to those who had shared with him the suffering of war, and whose affectionately loyal support had strengthened him in times of deep anxiety, the iron composure of the soldier was overcome by the heartfelt emotion of the man. Turning to his friends, he said, "With a heart full of love and gratitude, I now take leave of you, most devoutly wishing that your latter days may be as prosperous and happy as your former ones have been glorious and honorable."

In tones broken by overpowering feeling, the Commander made a last request: "I cannot come to each of you to take my leave, but shall be obliged if each of you will come and take me by the hand." The nearest and the first to come was General Knox. Washington silently grasped his hand and affectionately embraced him. The tears of each man hallowed his farewell.

In severing his connection with the army Washington stopped in Philadelphia to present his accounts to the comptroller of the treasury. They were in perfect order, in his own handwriting, from the time of his departure to take command at Cambridge. The amount to July 1, 1783, was 1972 pounds, 9 shillings, and 4 pence. It included the traveling expenses of Mrs. Washington between headquarters and Mount Vernon each winter, and large sums for secret information in connection with each campaign. Washington asked nothing for his own service.

After his return to Mount Vernon, Washington's thoughts frequently reverted to his comrades-in-arms. One of his first letters, after a short period of absolute retirement, expresses the feelings with which he resumed the peaceful life of a farmer. It was to Lafayette, saying:

"At length, my dear Marquis, I am become a private citizen on the banks of the Potomac, and, under the shadow of my own vine and my own fig-tree, free from the bustle of a camp and the busy scenes of public life.

I am solacing myself with those tranquil enjoyments, of which the soldier, who is ever in pursuit of fame, the statesman, whose watchful days and sleepless nights are spent in devising schemes to promote the welfare of his own, perhaps the ruin of other countries, as if this globe was insufficient for us all, and the courtier, who is always watching the countenance of his prince, in hopes of catching a gracious smile, can have very little conception. I have not only retired from all public employments, but I am retiring within myself, and shall be able to view the solitary walk, and tread the paths of private life, with a heartfelt satisfaction. Envious of none, I am determined to be pleased with all; and this, my dear friend, being the order of my march, I will move gently down the stream of life, until I sleep with my fathers."

A short time later he wrote to the Marquise de Lafayette inviting her to visit Mount Vernon and "call my cottage your home."

To General Knox, Washington wrote, "Strange as it may seem, it is nevertheless true that it was not till lately I could get the better of my usual custom of ruminating, as soon as I waked in the morning, on the business of the ensuing day; and of my surprise at finding, after revolving many things in my mind, that I was no longer a public man, nor had anything to do with public transactions.

"I feel now, however, as I conceive a wearied traveler must do, who, after treading many a painful step with a heavy burthen on his shoulders, is eased of the latter, having reached the haven to which all the former were directed; and from his house-top is looking back, and tracing with an eager eye the meanders by which he escaped the quicksand and mires which lay in his way; and into which none but the all-powerful Guide and Dispenser of human events could have prevented his falling."

The spring of 1784 brought a throng of visitors to Mount Vernon, both military and civil. The most distinguished and one of the most joyfully welcomed was Lafayette, so endeared to Washington by the most affectionately loyal service, and so valued in the negotiations with France and the delicate establishment of rapport with De Grasse and Rochambeau at a most critical moment.

Immediately upon his retirement to Mount Vernon, Washington began to improve the management of his farms by the importation of new seeds, new implements, and new methods of cultivation. He carried on a long correspondence with Arthur Young, a very practical and successful English farmer, evidently finding great satisfaction in the exchange of ideas and seeds.

Sparks's review of Washington's farming activities is comprehensive: "The first year after the war he applied himself mainly to farming operations, with the view of restoring his neglected fields and commencing a regular system of practical agriculture. He gradually abandoned the cultivation of tobacco, which exhausted his lands, and substituted wheat and grass as better suited to the soil, and in the aggregate more profitable. He began a new method of rotation of crops, in which he studied the particular qualities of the soil in the different parts of his farms, causing wheat, maize, potatoes, oats, grass, and other crops to succeed each other in the same field at stated times. So exact was he in this method that he drew out a scheme in which all his fields were numbered, and the crops assigned to them for several years in advance. It proved so successful that he pursued it to the end of his life, with occasional slight deviations by way of experiment.

"Having thus arranged and systematized his agricultural operations, he now set himself at work in earnest to execute his purpose of planting and adorning the grounds around the mansion-house. In the direction of the left wing, and at a considerable distance, was a vegetable garden; and on the right, at an equal distance, was another garden for ornamental shrubs, plants, and flowers. Between these gardens, in front of the house, was a spacious lawn, surrounded by serpentine walks. Beyond the gardens and lawn were the orchards. Very early in the spring he began with the lawn, selecting the choicest trees from the woods on his estates, and transferring them to the borders of the serpentine walks, arranging them in such a manner as to produce symmetry and beauty in the general effect, intermingling in just proportions forest trees, evergreens, and flowering shrubs. He attended personally to the selection, removal, and planting of every tree; and his *Diary* proves that he engaged in it with intense interest, and anxiously watched each tree and shoot till it showed signs of renewed growth. Such trees as were not found on his own lands he obtained from other parts of the country, and at length his design was completed according to his wishes.

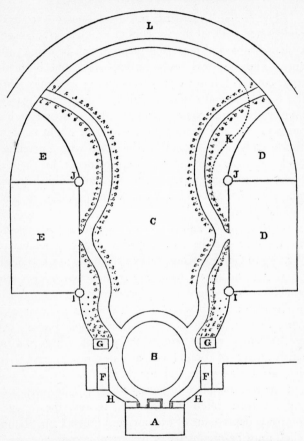

PLAN OF THE MANSION AND GROUNDS AT MOUNT VERNON

A—the Mansion
B—oval grass-plot
C—the lawn
DD—flower-garden
EE—vegetable garden
FF—kitchen and laundry

GG—house-servants' quarters
HH—circular colonnades
JJ—seed-houses
K—carriage-way as finally
    laid out
L—outside road

"The orchards, gardens, and green-houses were next replenished with all the varieties of rare fruit-trees, vegetables, shrubs, and flowering plants which he could procure. This was less easily accomplished; but horticulture being with him a favorite pursuit, he continued during his life to make new accessions of fruits and plants, both native and exotic. Pruning trees was one of his amusements; and in the proper season he might be seen almost daily in his grounds and gardens with a pruning-hook or other horticultural implement in his hands. Skillful gardeners were sought by him from Europe, whose knowledge and experience enabled him to execute his plans."

At this time Washington's correspondence in general became such that he was obliged to engage a secretary. Writing to General Knox, he explained the need, saying: "It is not the letters from my friends which give me trouble, or add aught to my perplexity. It is reference to old matters with which I have nothing to do; applications which oftentimes cannot be complied with; inquiries which would require the pen of a historian to satisfy; letters of compliment, as unmeaning, perhaps, as they are troublesome, but which must be attended to; and the commonplace business, which employs my pen and my time, often disagreeably. Indeed, these, with company, deprive me of exercise, and unless I can obtain relief, must be productive of disagreeable consequences."

Washington obtained the relief from this form of drudgery in the services of young Tobias Lear, who had won honors at Harvard College. He was engaged to begin the education of Nellie Custis and her younger brother, who was then known as little Washington. As no strenuous demands were ever laid upon the Custis children, young Lear was able to give the General much help in a secretarial capacity. He became greatly beloved in the family and a lifelong friend. After two years of residence under the Washington roof, Lear expressed his convictions to a friend: "General Washington is, I believe, almost the only man of an exalted character who does not lose some part of his respectability by an intimate acquaintance. I have never found a single thing that could lessen my respect for him. A complete knowledge of his honesty, uprightness, and candor in all his private transactions has sometimes led me to think him more than a man."

It was inevitable that Washington should be consulted by men engaged in shaping the political destiny of the infant republic. To all matters broached, Washington gave deliberate consideration. Writing to John Jay, in August, 1786, he said, "I do not conceive we can long exist as a nation, without having lodged somewhere a power which will pervade the whole Union in as energetic a manner as the authority of the state governments extends over the several states. To be fearful of investing Congress with powers, constituted as that body is, appears to me the very climax of popular absurdity and madness. Could Congress exert them for the detriment of the public without injuring themselves in an equal or greater proportion? Are not their interests inseparably connected with those of their constituents?"

During the deliberations of the Constitutional Convention in Philadelphia, Washington wrote, under date of August 15, 1787, "Thirteen governments pulling against each other, and all tugging at the federal head, will soon bring ruin on the whole; whereas a liberal and energetic constitution, well checked and well watched, to prevent encroachments, might restore us to that degree of respectability and consequence to which we had the fairest prospect of attaining."

In the Constitutional Convention Washington again found himself surrounded, as in the first Continental Congress, with the most brilliant minds of the country. Some had been members of that first congress, and some had signed the Declaration of Independence. Hamilton and Madison were two of the younger members who had not yet gathered their brightest laurels. But whereas in the first Congress Washington had been one of the more silent and inconspicuous members, he was now the acknowledged leader, to whom all deferred.

Sparks informs us that Washington went to preside at the Convention after much study. "His knowledge of the institutions of his country and of its political forms, both in their general character and minute affiliated relations, gained by inquiry and long experience, was probably as complete as that of any other man. But he was not satisfied with this alone. He read the history and examined the principles of the ancient and modern confederacies. There is a paper in his handwriting which contains an abstract of each, and in which are noted, in a methodical order, their chief characteristics, the kinds of authority they possess, their modes of operation, and their defects. The confederacies analyzed in this paper are Lycian, Amphictyonic, Achaian, Helvetic, Belgic, and

Germanic. He also read the standard works on general politics and the science of government, abridging parts of them, according to his usual practice, that he might impress the essential points more deeply on his mind."

After so much study it is not a matter of wonder that Benjamin Franklin was able to glance with satisfaction at the chair occupied by Washington during the session of the convention. Upon the back of the chair was painted a radiant sun, causing the philosopher to remark: "I have often and often, in the course of the session, and the vicissitudes of my hopes and fears as to its issue, looked at that sun behind the president, without being able to tell whether it was rising or setting; at length I have the happiness to know it is a rising, not a setting sun."

Washington wrote in his diary, on the day following the adjournment of the Convention, "The business being thus closed, the members adjourned to the City Tavern, dined together, and took a cordial leave of each other; after which I returned to my lodgings, did some business with, and received the papers from, the secretary of the Convention, and retired to meditate on the momentous work which had been executed, after not less than five, for a large part of the time, six, and sometimes seven hours' sitting every day (except Sundays, and the ten days' adjournment to give a committee an opportunity and time to arrange the business) for more than four months."

CHAPTER XIV

THE PRESIDENT

Before the Constitution had been adopted Alexander Hamilton had foreseen the inevitable.

"If the government be adopted," he wrote, "it is probable that General Washington will be the president of the United States. This will insure a wise choice of men to administer the government, and a good administration. A good administration will conciliate the confidence and affection of the people, and perhaps enable the government to acquire more consistency than the proposed constitution seems to promise for so great a country."

To Governor Trumbull, of Connecticut, Washington wrote in December, 1788: "May Heaven assist me in forming a judgment; for at present I see nothing but clouds and darkness before me. This much I may safely say to you in confidence: if ever I should, from any apparent necessity, be induced to go from home in a public character again, it will certainly be the greatest sacrifice of feelings and happiness that ever was or ever can be made by me."

The following April he was officially notified of his election. He was obliged to bid farewell to his mother, as both realized that her days were numbered. She was more than fourscore years of age, and afflicted with an incurable malady. He left her well provided for, and under the tender eye of her only daughter, Mrs. Fielding Lewis, who lived near her.

Washington's journey from Mount Vernon to New York, to take office, was a continuous ovation. He was hailed at every village and crossroads. At every town he was met by deputations of prominent citizens, who escorted him to the next town. In the larger cities decorated arches were prepared for him to pass under, and he was tumultuously escorted into the city of New York. Washington Irving, who saw him step out upon the balcony of Federal Hall to take the oath of office, says: "He was hailed by universal shouts. He was evidently moved by the demonstration of public affection. Advancing to the front of the balcony, he laid his hand upon his heart, bowed several times, and then retreated to an arm-chair near the table. The populace appeared to understand that the scene had overcome him, and were hushed at once into profound silence."

Washington soon found himself besieged by visitors of every description. Writing to a friend, Dr. Stuart, he said, "By the time I had done breakfast, and thence till dinner, and afterwards till bed-time, I could not get rid of the ceremony of one visit before I had to attend to another. In a word, I had no leisure to read or answer the dispatches that were pouring in upon me from all quarters." With characteristic method, he proceeded to set a time for visits, though only after consultation with Vice-President Adams and others.

Custis, commenting upon Washington's love of order, says: "Wherever Washington established a home— whether temporary or fixed, whether amid the log huts of Morristown or the Valley Forge, the presidential mansions in New York or Philadelphia, or his own beloved Mount Vernon—everywhere order, method, punctuality, economy reigned. His household, whether civil or military, was always upon a liberal scale, and was conducted with due regard to economy and usefulness.

"The public days of the first president of the United States were two in each week. On Tuesdays, from three to four o'clock, a levee was held for foreign ministers, strangers, and others, who could there be presented to the chief magistrate without the formality of letters of introduction. . . . Plain in all his habits, there was none to whom the details of official parade and ceremony could be less desirable; but correct in all his varied stations of life, the days of the first presidency will ever appear as among the most dignified and imposing in our country's annals.

"On Thursday the president gave his congressional and diplomatic dinners; and on Friday night Mrs. Washington received company in what was then, and is still, called the drawing-room."

Washington was aware of criticisms of the style in which he lived, and in a letter to Dr. Stuart declared, "These visits are optional; they are made without invitation. . . . Gentlemen, often in great numbers, come and go, chat with each other, and act as they please. A porter shows them into the room, and they retire from it when they choose, without ceremony. At their first entrance they salute me, and I them, and as many as I can, I talk to. What 'pomp' there is in all this I am unable to discover."

The letter of a Colonel Stone describes Mrs. Washington's drawing-rooms: "There was no place for the intrusion of the rabble in crowds, or for the mere coarse and boisterous partisan. There was no place for the vulgar electioneer or impudent place-hunter. On the contrary, they were select, and more courtly than have been given by any of Washington's successors. Proud of her husband's exalted fame, and jealous of the honors due, not only to his own lofty character, but to the dignified station to which a grateful country had called him, Mrs. Washington was careful, in her drawing-rooms, to exact those courtesies to which she knew he was entitled, as well on account of personal merit as of official consideration. None, therefore, were admitted to the levees but those who had either a right by official station to be there, or were entitled to the privilege by established merit and character."

The picture of Mrs. Washington's drawing-room is further illuminated by her own grandson, the ever-delightful Custis, whom it is a pleasure to quote:

"When Mrs. Washington received company it was on Friday, commencing about seven, and ending about nine o'clock. Two rooms were thrown open. The furniture that was thought handsome in those days would be considered barely decent in modern times. The principal ornament was a glass chandelier in the largest room, burning wax lights. The chair of the lady of the president was a plain arm-chair lined with green morocco leather.

"The ladies visiting the drawing-room were always attended by gentlemen. It was not the habit for very

young girls to be present at the drawing-room, but only
those of the age when it is proper for ladies to go into
company. Upon the ladies being introduced they were
seated, and the President, who always attended the drawing-room, passed round the circle, paying his respects to
each in succession; and it was a common remark, among
the chit-chat of the drawing-room, that the Chief was no
inconsiderable judge of female beauty, since he was
observed to tarry longer than usual when paying his
compliments to Miss Sophia Chew, a charming belle of
Philadelphia in that time.

"Refreshments were handed round by servants in
livery; and about that period first appeared the luxury,
now so universal, of ice-cream. Introductions to eminent
personages and conversation formed the entertainments
of the drawing-room. Cards were altogether unknown.

"But the leading and most imposing feature of the
drawing-room was the men of mark, the 'Revolution-
aries,' both civil and military, who were to be seen there.
The old officers delighted to pay their respects to the
wife of Washington, and to call up the reminiscences
of the headquarters. These glorious old chevaliers were
the greatest beaux of the age, and the recollections of
their gallant achievements, together with their elegant
manners, made them acceptable to the ladies everywhere.
They formed the élite of the drawing-rooms. General
Wayne, the renowned 'Mad Anthony,' with his aids-de-
camp, Lewis and De Butts, frequently attended, with
Mifflin, Walter Stewart, Colonel Hartley, and many
others. Indeed, there was often to be met with at the
mansion of the first president an assemblage of intellect

and honor, public virtue and private worth, exalted merit and illustrious services, such as the world will never see again."

It was in mid-summer of 1789 that Washington was afflicted with an illness which Lossing describes as a "malignant anthrax or carbuncle." Sparks says: "He was confined six weeks to his bed, and it was more than twelve before his strength was restored. . . . From the effects of it he never entirely recovered."

Washington himself, on the eighth of September, wrote to Doctor Craik, saying, "Though now freed from pain, the wound given by the incision is not yet healed." This is said to have been the most painful illness of his life. Custis names the president's disorder a *malignant carbuncle,* saying, in the next breath, "The painful tumor was upon his thigh, and was brought on by the excitements and labors which he had undergone since his inauguration." He also says, "Being left alone with his physician, the sufferer, looking him steadily in the face, desired his candid opinion as to the probable termination of the disease, adding, with perfect composure, 'Do not flatter me with vain hopes; I am not afraid to die, and therefore can bear the worst.' Dr. Bard expressed a hope, but acknowledged his apprehensions. Washington replied, with the same coolness, 'Whether tonight or twenty years hence makes no difference. I know that I am in the hands of a good Providence.'"

The death of his mother occurred before Washington had fully recovered from his own severe illness. She expired at the age of eighty-two years, at Fredericksburg, surrounded by her daughter's family.

One of the great responsibilities which confronted Washington on his accession to office was the choice of executives to administer the affairs of the new republic. Innumerable applications for the various offices were made to him. Sparks quotes a letter written to a gentleman who had solicited an office for another person. It indicates the principles which governed him in making appointments. "So far as I know my own heart," he wrote, "I would not be in the remotest degree influenced in making nominations by motives arising from the ties of family of blood; and that, on the other hand, three things, in my opinion, ought principally to be regarded, namely, the fitness of characters to fill offices, the comparative claims from the former merits and sufferings in service of the different candidates, and the distribution of appointments in as equal a proportion as might be to persons belonging to the different states in the Union. Without precautions of this kind I clearly foresaw the endless jealousies, and possibly the fatal consequences, to which a government, depending altogether on the good-will of the people for its establishment, would certainly be exposed in its early stages. Besides, I thought, whatever the effect might be in pleasing or displeasing any individuals at the present moment, a due concern for my own reputation, not less decisively than a sacred regard to the interests of the community, required that I should hold myself absolutely at liberty to act, while in office, with a sole reference to justice and the public good."

These principles were exemplified in the choice of Alexander Hamilton to direct the treasury, a choice

which is said to have been made with the recommendation of Robert Morris, the "financier of the Revolution."
At the sacrifice of private interests the office was accepted
by Hamilton in the conviction that "it is the situation in
which I can do the most good." It is well known that he
undertook the difficult task in the firm belief that he
would be able to restore the public credit, then in a
deplorable condition.

General Henry Knox was chosen for the office of
secretary of war.

Writing to Mr. John Jay, requesting him to assume
the responsibilities of the chief justiceship of the United
States, Washington said: "I have a full confidence that
the love which you bear to our country, and a desire to
promote the general happiness, will not suffer you to
hesitate a moment to bring into action the talents, knowledge, and integrity which are so necessary to be exercised
at the head of that department which must be considered
the keystone of our political fabric."

Believing Thomas Jefferson's long and varied service
at home and abroad* of inestimable value, Washington
selected him as secretary of state. To Jefferson the president wrote, "In the selection of characters to fill the
important offices of government I was naturally led to
contemplate the talents and disposition which I knew
you to possess and entertain for the service of the country,
and without being able to consult your inclination, or to
derive any knowledge of your intentions from your letters either to myself or to any of your friends, I was

---

* In 1784 Jefferson, Franklin, and Adams were in Europe making
financial treaties. The following year Jefferson succeeded Franklin as
foreign minister to France.

determined, as well by motives of private regard as a conviction of public propriety, to nominate you for the department of state, which, under its present organization, involves many of the most interesting objects of the executive authority."

After his tour through the New England states, made for the purpose of acquainting himself more thoroughly with the conditions in that part of the country, Washington followed with close concentration the assumption by the government of the national and state debts. On this legislation we quote from Marshall: "The effect of the measure was great and rapid. The public paper suddenly rose, and was for a short time above par. The immense wealth which individuals acquired by this unexpected appreciation could not be viewed with indifference. Those who participated in its advantages regarded the author of a system to which they were so greatly indebted with an enthusiasm of attachment to which scarcely any limits were assigned. To many others this adventitious collection of wealth in particular hands was a subject rather of chagrin than of pleasure; and the reputation which the success of his plans gave to the secretary of the treasury was not contemplated with unconcern."

This condition marked the beginning of the dissensions between Hamilton and Jefferson, which later caused Washington so much trouble. Himself without jealousy, Washington was unable to foresee it among others. He wrote to Lafayette, "Many of your old acquaintances and friends are concerned with me in the administration of this government. By having Mr. Jefferson at the head of the department of state, Mr. Jay of the judiciary, Hamilton of the treasury, and Knox of war, I feel myself supported by able coadjutors who harmonize extremely well."

Another illness, designated by Lossing as "inflammation of the lungs" menaced the life of Washington in the spring of 1790. The sea-voyage he made, accompanied by Jefferson, to Newport, Rhode Island, restored his health.

The financial prosperity of the country seemed to justify the measures of the governmental financial policy, and Hamilton now pressed his plan for a national bank. This measure was strenuously opposed by Jefferson, who included Washington in the unwarrantable statements which he leveled against his political opponent in the treasury. The measure passed, however, and later Mr. Jefferson's proposed decimal system of coinage was adopted by the country.

Washington's own estimate of his personal value to the infant government is expressed in a letter written to Lafayette in May, 1791, when he wrote: "I wish it were in my power to give you an assurance that our troubles are at an end, and our Constitution totally established. But, although dark clouds are still before us, we have come so far as to foresee the moment when the legislative corps will succeed this convention; and, unless foreign powers interfere, I hope that within four months your friend will have resumed the life of a private and quiet citizen. The rage of parties, even among the patriots, is gone as far as it is possible, short of blood-shed; but, although hatreds are far from subsiding, matters do not appear so much disposed as they formerly were toward collision among the supporters of the popular cause. I myself am exposed to the envy and attacks of all parties—for this simple reason, that whoever acts or means wrong finds me an insuperable obstacle. And there appears a kind of phenomenon in my situation—all parties against me, and a national popularity, which, in spite of every effort, has remained unchanged. . . . Given up to all the madness of license, faction, and popular rage, I stood alone in defense of the law, and turned the tide into the constitutional channel."

In the spring of 1791 Washington undertook a tour through the Southern states. The mode of travel of the time is indicated by an entry in his diary: "I was accompanied by Major Jackson. My equipage and attendants consisted of a chariot and four horses drove in hand, a light baggage-wagon and two horses, four saddle-horses, besides a led one for myself; and five, to wit, my valet-de-chambre, two footmen, coachman, and postillion." He was showered with honors at every turn.

Upon his return to Philadelphia, the seat of government having been removed to that city, Washington wrote to Colonel Humphreys, then in Paris, saying, "I am much pleased that I have undertaken the journey, as it has enabled me to see with my own eyes the situation of the country through which we traveled, and to learn more accurately the disposition of the people than I could from any information. The country appears to be in a very improving state, and industry and frugality are becoming much more fashionable than they have hitherto been. Tranquillity reigns among the people, with that disposition toward the general government which is likely to preserve it. They begin to feel the good effects of equal laws and equal protection. The farmer finds a ready market for his produce, and the merchant calculates with more certainty on his payments. Manufactures have as yet made but little progress in that part of the country, and it will probably be a long time before they are brought to that state to which they have already arrived in the middle and eastern parts of the Union. Each day's experience of the government of the United States seems to confirm its establishment, and to make it more popular. A ready acquiescence in the laws made under it shows in a strong light the confidence which the people have in their representatives, and in the upright views of those who administer the government.

"Our public credit stands on that ground which, three years ago, it would have been a species of madness to have foretold. The astonishing rapidity with which the newly-instituted bank was filled gives an unexampled proof of the resources of our countrymen and their confidence in public measures. On the first day of opening the subscription, the whole number of shares (twenty thousand) were taken up in one hour, and application made for upwards of four thousand shares more than were granted by the institution, besides many others that were coming in from different quarters."

One of the difficulties of the first administration was

with the Indians. Sparks writes of this: "During the war the Indians on the borders of the United States had almost everywhere been allied with the enemy. When peace came, it found them in the attitude of hostility, their savage spirit roused, and their vindictive tempers eager for slaughter and revenge; and the United States were left to appease and conciliate them as they could. In any case this would have been an arduous task, but the difficulty was soon perceived to be increased by a foreign influence keeping alive their enmity, and stimulating them to acts of outrage. British agents and traders on the northern frontier furnished the Indians with arms, ammunition, and clothing. In Florida the Spaniards tampered with the Creeks and other southern Indians, and kept them at variance with their white neighbors. These acts were not acknowledged, possibly not authorized, by the English and Spanish governments, but they were certainly not restrained, and they were repeated long after full representations had been made.

"The effect was a protracted and expensive war. Washington's policy in regard to the Indians was always pacific and humane. He considered them as children, who should be treated with tenderness and forbearance. He aimed to conciliate them by good usage, to obtain their lands by fair purchase and punctual payments, to make treaties with them on terms of equity and reciprocal advantages, and strictly to redeem every pledge. In these respects he looked upon the Indian tribes as holding the same rank and the same rights as civilized nations, but their faithlessness, ravages, and murders were not to be tolerated, from whatever causes they arose. After failing in every attempt at a pacification, he was convinced that war was the only alternative. It continued four or five years, with many vicissitudes of misfortune and disaster, the defeats of Harmar and St. Clair, unsuccessful campaigns, and much waste of blood and treasure, till General Wayne put an end to it, first by a battle, and then by a treaty of peace. This war lasted through a large part of Washington's administration. It was a source of regret and pain to him, on account both of its cause, the necessity of subduing by force the turbulence of an ignorant and deluded race of men, and of the heavy charge it imposed on the nation for maintaining an army."

We turn to Custis for an account of the powerful emotional reaction of the president on hearing of St. Clair's defeat. It appears that Washington controlled his feelings in the presence of his family, but later released them when left alone with his secretary. Custis, at the time, was a boy of about ten years of age, and undoubtedly had from Colonel Lear the account given below. It agrees with that presented by the Honorable Richard Rush, who had access to Colonel Lear's diary and private correspondence.

Custis is quoted: "The president was dining when an officer arrived from the western army with dispatches, his orders requiring that he should deliver them only to the Commander-in-chief. The president retired, but soon reappeared, bearing in his hand an open letter. No change was perceptible in his countenance, as, addressing the company, he observed that the army of St. Clair had been surprised by the Indians, and was cut to pieces. The company soon after retired. The president repaired to his private parlor, attended by Mr. Lear, his principal secretary, and a scene ensued of which our pen can give but a feeble description.

"The chief paced the room in hurried strides. In his agony he struck his clenched hands with fearful force against his forehead, and in a paroxysm of anguish exclaimed: 'That brave army, so officered—Butler, Ferguson, Kirkwood—such officers are not to be replaced in a day—that brave army cut to pieces! O God!' Then turning to the secretary, who stood amazed at a spectacle so unique as Washington in all his terrors, he continued: 'It was here, sir, in this very room, that I conversed with St. Clair, on the very eve of his departure for the West. I remarked, "I shall not interfere, General, with the orders of General Knox and the war department; they are sufficiently comprehensive and judicious; but, as an old soldier, as one whose early life was particularly engaged in Indian warfare, I feel myself competent to counsel; General St. Clair, in three words, beware of surprise; trust not the Indian; leave not your arms for a moment; and when you halt for the night, be sure to fortify your camp—again and again, General, beware of surprise." And yet that brave army surprised, and cut to pieces, with Butler, and a host of others, slain! O God!' Here the struggle ended, as with mighty efforts the hero chained down the rebellious giant of passion, and Washington became himself again. In a subdued tone of voice he proceeded: 'But he shall have justice; yes, long, faithful, and meritorious services have their claims. I repeat—*he shall have justice!'*

"Thus concluded a scene as remarkable as rare. It served to display this great man as nature had made him, with passion fierce and impetuous, which, like the tornado of the tropics, would burst for a while in awful grandeur, and then show, in higher relief, a serene and brilliant sky."

It is said that Custis was present at the meeting which he thus describes: "The first interview of the president with St. Clair, after the fatal fourth of November (1791), was nobly impressive. The unfortunate general, worn down by age, disease, and the hardships of a frontier campaign, assailed by the press, and with the current of popular opinion setting hard against him, repaired to his Chief as to a shelter from the fury of so many elements. Washington extended his hand to one who appeared in no new character; for, during the whole of a long life, misfortune seemed to have marked him for her own. Poor old St. Clair hobbled up to his Chief, seized the offered hand in both of his, and gave vent to his feelings in an audible manner. He was subsequently tried by a commission of government, and proved to have been *unfortunate."*

The strain of office was severely felt by Washington at this time, and he consulted the members of his cabinet as to the propriety of resigning. Jefferson and Hamilton concurring in their advice to him to continue his labors for the common good, he gave his consent to re-election.

His administration had been clouded by the growing discord between the two men, each an able and conscientious executive in his own department, but so antagonistic to the other as to defeat all Washington's efforts to create harmony between them. He wrote many long, earnest letters to each of them, all expressive of the one thought which closed a letter to Jefferson: "I have a great, a sincere, esteem and regard for you both, and ardently wish that some line may be marked out by which both of you could walk." Being unable to heal the breach, Washington was resigned to curb their hostility as much as possible by his influence. He had made a noble attempt to effect the impossible.

CHAPTER XV

THE SECOND TERM

For some time Washington had treasured a grim souvenir of growing republicanism in France. It was the key to the Bastile, which had been sent to him by Lafayette, himself an ardent reformer, after the storming of the French state prison on July 14, 1789. The movement for constitutional government in France having acquired a ferocious and sanguine character quite at variance with the idealistic principles of Lafayette, he felt obliged to seek asylum in Holland until the Reign of Terror should abate. On his way he was detained at Rochefort, the first Austrian post, and later imprisoned in a dungeon at Olmutz.

Gouverneur Morris, who had been appointed minister to France after Mr. Jefferson's resignation of the post, wrote to Washington, "We have had a week of unchecked murders in which thousands have perished in this city. It began with two or three hundred of the clergy. . . . All those who were confined either on the accusation or suspicion of crimes were destroyed."

Washington was grieved to hear of Lafayette's fate, and wished to befriend his wife and young children. Immediately upon being informed of their probable residence, he wrote to the Marquise as follows: "If I had words that could convey to you an adequate idea of my feelings on the present situation of the Marquis de

Lafayette, this letter would appear to you in a different garb. The sole object in writing to you now is to inform you that I have deposited in the hands of Mr. Nicholas Van Staphorst, of Amsterdam, two thousand three hundred and ten guilders, Holland currency, equal to two hundred guineas, subject to your orders.

"This sum is, I am certain, the least I am indebted for services rendered to me by the Marquis de Lafayette, of which I never yet have received the account. I could add much; but it is best, perhaps, that I should say little on this subject. Your goodness will supply my deficiency.

"The uncertainty of your situation, after all the inquiries I have made, has occasioned a delay in this address and remittance; and even now, the measure adopted is more the effect of a desire to find where you are than from any knowledge I have obtained of your residence."

Soon after sending this letter Washington received one from the Marquise, sent from Chavaniac, where she was a prisoner in ignorance of the fate of her husband. "He was taken," she wrote, "by the troops of the emperor, although the king of Prussia retains him a prisoner in his dominions. And while he suffers this inconceivable persecution from the enemies without, the faction which reigns within keeps me a hostage at one hundred and twenty leagues from the capital. Judge, then, at what distance I am from him. In this abyss of misery, the idea of owing to the United States and to Washington the life and liberty of M. de Lafayette kindles a ray of hope in my heart. I hope everything from the goodness of the people with whom he has set an example of that liberty of which he is now made the victim."

The letter closed with a desire of the Marquise to share her husband's exile. Washington was powerless to aid his friends, except in giving instructions to American ministers abroad to make every effort to secure the release of the prisoner.

Sparks explains the inability of Washington to act in the matter: "The United States had neither authority to make demands, nor power to enforce them. They had no immediate intercourse with Prussia or Austria, and were in no condition to ask the favors or avenge the tyranny of the rulers of those countries, who were only responsible for the treatment of Lafayette, and whose pleasure it was, if not their policy and interest, to keep him in chains."

At length the wife and daughter of Lafayette were allowed to share his exile, and his son, George Washington Lafayette, came to America.

Jefferson's attacks upon Hamilton continued to distress Washington, who had an abiding faith in the secretary of the treasury. Hamilton himself answered all charges by formal reports of his conduct of his affairs, but opposition became still more bitter.

It was cares such as these that weighed upon the president and caused him to write to Colonel Humphreys, "At my age the love of retirement grows every day more and more powerful, and the death of my nephew will, I apprehend, cause my private concerns to suffer very much."

This nephew was George Augustine Washington, son of the president's brother, Charles. George was married to Fanny Bassett, a niece of Mrs. Washington. He had fought in the Revolution. The General had a strong affection for young George Augustine, and when his health failed, provided him with the means to go to the West Indies. The young man improved and returned to Mount Vernon, where the General employed him as manager of his estate to succeed Lund Washington, who had retired, though under the General's protest. A romance ensued between George Augustine and pretty Fanny, and they continued to live at Mount Vernon following their marriage. A return of the malady caused the General great anxiety and necessitated George Augustine's retirement.

To Lafayette, Washington had written as early as June, 1792: "I am afraid my nephew George, your old aid, will never have his health perfectly re-established. He has lately been attacked with the alarming symptoms of spitting large quantities of blood, and the physicians give no hope of restoration, unless it can be effected by a change of air and a total dereliction from business, to which he is too anxiously attentive. He will, if he should be taken from his family and friends, leave three fine children, two sons and a daughter. To the eldest of the boys he has given the name of Fayette, and a fine-looking child he is."

To General Knox he wrote: "I thank you most sincerely for the medicine you were so obliging as to send for my nephew, and for the sympathetic feeling you express for his situation. Poor fellow; neither, I believe, will be of any avail. Present appearances indicate a speedy dissolution. He has not been able to leave his bed, except for a few moments to sit in an arm-chair, since the fourteenth or fifteenth of last month. The paroxysm of the disorder seems to be upon him, and death, or a favorable turn to it, must speedily follow."

The sufferer was then residing upon a small estate in Hanover. He lingered for several weeks, and then expired; and on the twenty-fourth of February Washington wrote to his widow: "My dear Fanny: To you, who so well knew the affectionate regard I had for our departed friend, it is unnecessary to describe the sorrow with which I was afflicted at the news of his death, although it was an event I had expected many weeks before it happened. To express this sorrow with the force I feel it would answer no other purpose than to revive in your breast that poignancy of anguish, which by this time I hope is abated. The object of this letter is to convey to your mind the warmest assurance of my love, friendship, and disposition to serve you. These I also profess to bear in an eminent degree for your children."

Washington then invited the young widow to make Mount Vernon the home of herself and children. "You can go to no place," he said, "where you will be more welcome, nor to any where you can live at less expense or trouble."

Fanny Washington appears to have declined the offer of a home at Mount Vernon, preferring to keep house in Alexandria, but she offered to resign the charge of her eldest son, Fayette, into Washington's keeping. In March the President wrote to her, saying: "The carriage which I sent to Mount Vernon for your use I never intended to reclaim, and now, making you a formal present of it, it may be sent for whenever it suits your convenience and be considered as your own. I shall, when I see you, request that Fayette may be given up to me, either at that time or as soon after as he is old enough to go to school. This will relieve you of the portion of attention which his education would otherwise call for."

Washington continued to extend his aid to Fanny until she terminated her widowhood by marrying his secretary, Colonel Tobias Lear, whose first wife, also a niece of Martha Washington, had died the year before in the president's home at Philadelphia, during the epidemic of yellow fever.

There was strong sympathy in America with the cause of the French Revolution, in spite of the brutalities which accompanied it. When France at length declared war upon England, a wave of sympathy swept the United States. Washington took a firm stand for neutrality in the conflict. Upon the arrival of "Citizen" Genêt, the people greeted him with enthusiastic demonstrations, leading him to believe that the whole American nation was friendly to France and antagonistic to her enemies. Lossing says: "He had come with secret instructions to foment war between the United States and England for the benefit of France, but that single interview with Washington made him feel, for the time, that his efforts must result in failure; for the word of the chief magistrate was yet almost as omnipotent as law with the greater portion of his countrymen."

Genêt's mischievous activities distressed Washington for some time, and even Jefferson, whose sentiments were so strongly republican, at length plainly objected to his "interference." Genêt's popularity declined as the people became convinced of the wisdom of Washington's course, and he was recalled.

Lossing tells of the unceasing efforts of Washington to secure the release of Lafayette, who for three years had been confined in a cell three paces broad and five and a half paces long.

"While Lafayette was in the hands of the Prussian authorities, John Marshall was sent to Berlin as a special and confidential agent to solicit his discharge. Before Marshall's arrival, Lafayette had been delivered by the king of Prussia into the hands of the emperor of Germany. Mr. Pinckney, the United States minister in London, was then instructed to indicate the wishes of the president concerning the prisoner, to the Austrian minister in England, and to solicit the powerful mediation of the British cabinet. These efforts failed, and Washington, disdaining to make further application to the deputies of sovereignty, whose petty tyranny was proverbial, determined to go to the fountain-head of power in the dominion where his friend was suffering, and, on the fifteenth of May, he wrote as follows to the emperor of Germany:

" 'It will readily occur to your Majesty that occasions may sometimes exist, on which official considerations would constrain the chief of a nation to be silent and passive in relation even to objects which affect his sensibility, and claim his interposition as a man. Finding myself precisely in this situation at present, I take the liberty of writing this private letter to your Majesty, being persuaded that my motives will also be my apology for it.

" 'In common with the people of this country, I retain a strong and cordial sense of the services rendered them by the Marquis de Lafayette; and my friendship for him has been constant and sincere. It is natural, therefore, that I should sympathize with him and his family in their misfortunes, and endeavor to mitigate the calamities which they experience; among which, his present confinement is not the least distressing.

" 'I forbear to enlarge on this delicate subject. Permit me only to submit to your Majesty's consideration, whether his long imprisonment, and the confiscation of his estates, and the indigence and dispersion of his family, and the painful anxieties incident to all these circumstances, do not form an assemblage of sufferings which recommend him to the mediation of humanity? Allow me, sir, on this occasion to be its organ, and to entreat that he may be permitted to come to this country, on such conditions, and under such restrictions, as your Majesty may think it expedient to prescribe.

" 'As it is a maxim with me not to ask what, under similar circumstances, I would not grant, your Majesty will do me the justice to believe that this request appears to me to correspond with those great principles of magnanimity and wisdom which form the basis of sound policy and durable glory.

" 'May the Almighty and Merciful Sovereign of the universe keep your Majesty under His protection and guidance.' "

This letter was transmitted to Mr. Pinckney, and by him sent to the emperor, through his minister in Great Britain. "How far it operated," says Marshall, "in mitigating immediately the rigor of Lafayette's confinement, or in obtaining his liberation, remains unascertained."

Perhaps the greatest political stress which Washington was compelled to undergo was the dissatisfaction following the Jay treaty with England, which was denounced in legislative sessions, in the newspapers, and in public and private gatherings. The political unrest of the times caused Washington to write to Patrick Henry, who was said to have some objections to the treaty:

"I persuade myself, sir, it has not escaped your observation that a crisis is approaching, that must, if it cannot be arrested, soon decide whether order and good government shall be preserved, or anarchy and confusion ensue. I can most religiously aver, I have no wish that is incompatible with the dignity, happiness, and true interest of the people of this country. My ardent desire is, and my aim has been, as far as depended upon the executive department, to comply strictly with all our engagements, foreign and domestic; but to keep the United States free from political connection with every other country, to see them independent of all, and under the influence of none. In a word, I want an *American* character, that the powers of Europe may be convinced we act for *ourselves,* and not for others. This, in my judgment, is the only way to be respected abroad and happy at home; and not, by becoming the partisans of Great Britain or France, create dissensions, disturb the public tranquillity, and destroy, perhaps forever, the cement which binds the Union."

It was at this inopportune moment that the son of Lafayette, then seventeen years old, was able to escape to

the United States (1795). The president, as such, believed it inexpedient to receive him at that time, lest
political affairs become further disturbed.

Young Lafayette, accompanied by his tutor, consigned
himself to the care of the president. Washington, though
yearning to treat the young man most tenderly, felt
obliged to place him at a distance from his own home.

His appeal to Senator Cabot of Boston, expresses his
difficulties: "To express all the sensibility which has been
excited in my breast by the receipt of young Lafayette's
letter, from the recollection of his father's merits, services,
and sufferings, from my friendship for him, and from
my wishes to become a friend and father to his son, is
unnecessary. Let me in a few words declare that I will
be his friend; but the manner of becoming so, considering
the obnoxious light in which his father is viewed by the
French government, and my own situation as the executive of the United States, requires more time to consider,
in all its relations, than I can bestow on it at present, the
letters not having been in my hands more than an hour,
and I myself on the point of setting out for Virginia to
fetch my family back, whom I left there about the first
of August.

"The mode which at the first view strikes me as the
most eligible to answer his purposes and to save appearances is, first, to administer all the consolation to the
young gentleman that he can derive from the most un-
equivocal assurances of my standing in the place of, and
becoming to him, a father, friend, protector, and sup-
porter. But, secondly, for prudential motives, as they
relate to myself, his mother and friends whom he has

left behind, and to my official character, it would be best not to make these sentiments public; and of course it would be ineligible that he should come to the seat of the general government, where all the foreign characters (particularly those of his own nation) are residents, until it is seen what opinions will be excited by his arrival; especially, too, as I shall be absent five or six weeks from it, on business in several places. Thirdly, considering how important it is to avoid idleness and dissipation, to improve his mind, and to give him all the advantages which education can bestow, my opinion and my advice to him are, if he is qualified for admission, that he should enter as a student in the university in Cambridge, although it should be for a short time only; the expense of which, as also for every other means for his support, I will pay. . . . Let me pray you, my dear sir, to impress upon young Lafayette's mind, and indeed upon that of his tutor, that the reasons why I do not urge him to come to me have been frankly related, and that their prudence must appreciate them with caution. My friendship for his father, so far from being diminished, has increased in the ratio of his misfortunes; and my inclination to serve the son will be evidenced by my conduct."

General Knox, then in Boston, took an interest in the exile and characterized him as "a lovely young man, of excellent morals and conduct." Writing to Washington, he said, "He goes by the name of Motier (a family name of his father), concealing his real name, lest some injury should arise to his mother, or to a young Mr. Russell of this town, now in France, who assisted in his escape."

It was impossible for young Lafayette to conceal his

identity at Cambridge, and he and his tutor accepted the invitation of a French gentleman to his country home near New York, until they should receive further directions from Washington.

Washington, upon his return to Philadelphia, wrote affectionately to young Lafayette, and also to his tutor, assuring that gentleman that he would provide "what he has occasion for."

Congress at length officially recognized the presence of the son of Lafayette in the country, and invited him to come to the capital. Thereupon Washington invited him to occupy a room in the presidential mansion, with the suggestion only that he avoid society as much as possible.

Washington's public service ending the following spring (1797), he bore the young exile to his own home, where he cherished him affectionately. Young Lafayette remained at Mount Vernon until October, when he received the news of his father's release and his return to France. The son immediately departed for France, bearing for his father a tender letter from Washington.

CHAPTER XVI

WASHINGTON AT HOME

Washington settled down on his beloved farm to enjoy its beauties and to relax from the anxieties of political life. In a letter to Mr. James McHenry, then secretary of war, he described his mode of life: "I might tell that I begin my diurnal course with the sun; that if my hirelings are not in their places at that time, I send them messages of sorrow for their indisposition; that, having put these wheels in motion, I examine the state of things further; that, the more they are probed, the deeper I find the wounds which my buildings have sustained by an absence and neglect of eight years; that, by the time I have accomplished these matters, breakfast (a little after seven o'clock, about the time I suppose you are taking leave of Mrs. McHenry) is ready; that, this being over, I mount my horse and ride round my farms, which employs me until it is time to dress for dinner, at which I rarely miss seeing strange faces—come, as they say, out of respect for me. Pray, would not the word *curiosity* answer as well? And how different this from having a few social friends at a cheerful board. The usual time of sitting at table, a walk, and tea, bring me within the dawn of candlelight; previous to which, if not prevented by company, I resolve that, as soon as the glimmering taper supplies the place of the great luminary, I will retire to my writing-table and acknowledge the letters I have received; but when the lights are brought, I feel tired, and disinclined to engage in this work, conceiving that the next will do as well. The next night comes, and with it the same causes for postponement, and so on.

"This will account for your letters remaining so long unacknowledged; and having given you the history of a day, it will serve for a year, and I am persuaded you will not require a second edition of it. But it may strike you that, in this detail, no mention is made of any portion of time allotted for reading. The remark would be just, for I have not looked into a book since I came home; nor shall I be able to do it until I have discharged my workmen, probably not before the nights grow longer, when possibly I shall be looking in Doomsday Book."

Washington soon found the entertainment of so many visitors very tiring, and wrote to his nephew, Lawrence Lewis, the son of his sister Betty: "As both your aunt and I are in the decline of life, and regular in our habits, especially in our hours of rising and going to bed, I require some person (fit and proper) to ease me of the trouble of entertaining company, particularly of nights, as it is my inclination to retire (and, unless prevented by very particular company, I always do retire) either to bed or to my study, soon after candle-light. In taking those duties (which hospitality obliges me to bestow on company) off my hands, it would render me a very acceptable service."

Young Lewis was glad to avail himself of his uncle's invitation, the more so as he was a great admirer of lovely Nelly Custis, Mrs. Washington's granddaughter, whom Washington had adopted on the death of her father at Yorktown. It was to Nelly that Washington had written a long letter on the indefinable emotion, love, when she was about sixteen. It was in reply to hers, telling him of her first ball.

"Dear Nelly:

"Your letter, the receipt of which I am now acknowledging, is written correctly and in fair characters, which is an evidence that you command, when you please, a fair hand. Possessed of these advantages, it will be your own fault if you do not avail yourself of them, and attention being paid to the choice of your subjects, you can have nothing to fear from the malignancy of criticism, as your ideas are lively, and your descriptions agreeable. Let me touch a little now on your Georgetown ball, and happy, thrice happy, for the fair who were assembled on the occasion, that there was a man to spare; for had there been seventy-nine ladies and only seventy-eight gentlemen, there might, in the course of the evening, have been some disorder among the caps; notwithstanding the apathy which *one* of the company entertains for the youth of the present day, and her determination 'never to give herself a moment's uneasiness on account of them.' A hint here: men and women feel the same inclinations to each other *now* that they always have done, and which they will continue to do until there is a new order of things, and *you,* as others have done, may find, perhaps, that the passions of your sex are easier raised than allayed. Do not, therefore, boast too soon or too strongly of your insensibility to, or resistance of, its powers. In the composition of the human frame there is a good deal of inflammable matter, however dormant it may lie for a time, and like an intimate acquaintance of yours, when the torch is put to it, *that* which is *within you* may burst into a blaze; for which reason, and especially, too, as I have entered upon the chapter of advices, I will read you a lecture drawn from this text.

"Love is said to be an involuntary passion, and it is, therefore, contended that it cannot be resisted. This is true in part only, for like all things else, when nourished and supplied plentifully with aliment, it is rapid in its progress; but let these be withdrawn and it may be stifled in its birth or much stinted in its growth. For example, a woman (the same may be said of the other sex), all beautiful and accomplished, will, while her hand and heart are undisposed of, turn the heads and set the circle in which she moves on fire. Let her marry, and what is the consequence? The madness *ceases,* and all is quiet again. Why? Not because there is any diminution in the charms of the lady, but because there is an end of hope. Hence it follows that love may and therefore ought to be under the guidance of reason, for although we cannot avoid first impressions, we may assuredly place them under guard; and my motives for treating on this subject are to show you, while you remain Eleanor Parke Custis, spinster, and retain the resolution to love with moderation, the propriety of adhering to the latter resolution, at least until you have secured your game, and the way by which it may be accomplished.

"When the fire is beginning to kindle, and your heart growing warm, propound these questions to it. Who is this invader? Have I a competent knowledge of him? Is he a man of good character? A man of sense? For, be assured, a sensible woman can never be happy with a fool. What has been his walk of life? Is he a gambler, a spend-thrift, or drunkard? Is his fortune sufficient to maintain me in the manner I have been accustomed to live, and my sisters do live, and is he one to whom my friends can have no reasonable objections? If these interroga-tories can be satisfactorily answered there will remain but one more to be asked; that, however, is an important one. Have I sufficient ground to conclude that his affections are engaged by me? Without this, the heart of sensibility will struggle against a passion that is not reciprocated—delicacy, custom, or call it by what epithet you will, having precluded all advances on your part. The declara-tion, without the *most indirect* invitation of yours, must proceed from the man, to render it permanent and valu-able, and nothing short of good sense and an easy, unaf-fected conduct can draw the line between prudery and coquetry. It would be no great departure from truth to say that it rarely happens otherwise than that a thor-ough-paced coquette dies in celibacy, as a punishment for her attempts to mislead others, by encouraging looks, words, or actions, given for no other purpose than to draw men on to make overtures that they may be rejected.

"This day, according to our information, gives a hus-band to your elder sister, and consummates, it is to be presumed, her fondest desires. The dawn with us is bright and propitious, I hope, of her future happiness, for a full measure of which she and Mr. Law have my earnest wishes. Compliments and congratulations, on this occasion, and best regards are presented to your mamma, Dr. Stuart, and family; and every blessing, among which a good husband when you want and deserve one, is bestowed on you by yours, affectionately."

That Nelly's younger brother, commonly called Washington, gave the General more concern than any possible "disorder among the caps" appears from the correspondence regularly carried on at a time when affairs of state were extremely absorbing. Even then, Washington made no effort to evade in the slightest, or to delegate to another, what he considered his duty to his adopted son. Doubtless the letters were among those penned by candle-light in the early morning before the day brought the succession of statesmen, diplomats, and military confreres who claimed his attention.

It is Nelly Custis who tells us that "Grandmama always spoiled Washington," meaning her brother. That the General constantly tried to awaken in the lad a feeling of responsibility and ambition to prepare himself for a life of usefulness and distinction is evidenced by the letters beginning with Custis's matriculation at Princeton. In true fatherly style Washington urges young Custis to "let no bad example, for such is to be met in all seminaries, have an improper influence upon your conduct. Let this be such, and let it be your pride, to demean yourself in such a manner as to obtain the good will of your superiors and the love of your fellow-students."

To one of the first letters the General appends a note, saying, "If you should meet with collegiate fare, remember it is unmanly to complain."

That the education of the young man did not proceed as the General wished it might is evinced by his letter to

Dr. Smith, head of the college at Princeton. The reason for it is probably a report of unsatisfactory progress in some course of study.

Mount Vernon, 24th May, 1797

"Reverend and dear Sir: Your favor of the 18th instant was received by the last post, the contents of which, relative to Mr. Custis, filled my mind (as you naturally supposed it would) with extreme disquietude. From his infancy I have discovered an almost unconquerable disposition to indolence in everything that did not tend to his amusements; and have exhorted him in the most parental and friendly manner, often, to devote his time to more useful pursuits. His pride has been stimulated, and his family expectations and wishes have been urged as inducements thereto. In short, I could say nothing to him now by way of admonition, encouragement, or advice that has not been repeated over and over again.

"It is my earnest desire to keep him to his studies as long as I am able, as well on account of the benefits he will derive from them, as for the purpose of excluding him from the company of idle and dissipated young men until his judgment is more matured.

"I can but thank you, sir, for your exertions to remove the error of his present thoughts, and I shall hope for your further endeavors to effect it. If you find, however, that the attempt will be in vain, I shall rely on your judgment to employ his time in such studies as you conceive will be most advantageous to him during his continuance with you, and I know of none more likely to prove so than those you have suggested, if his term at college will close with the next vacation. With very great esteem and regard, I am, reverend sir,

"Your most obedient and very humble servant,

"G. Washington."

Washington, however, did his young ward full justice in another letter, when placing him in St. John's College at Annapolis. Writing to the president he said, "From drinking and gaming he is perfectly free, and if he has a propensity to any other impropriety it is hidden from me. He is generous and regardful of the truth."

Washington always showed great interest in the welfare of each member of the Custis family of both generations. It was with regard to the mother of his namesake and adopted son that he had written, some years earlier, to Lund Washington, then in charge of Mount Vernon, who informed him that Dr. David Stuart, of Maryland, was a frequent visitor at Mount Vernon. Mrs. Custis, the first Nelly, was then an attractive widow, and Washington wrote concerning the rumored romance: "If this should be the case, and she wants advice upon it, a father and mother (Mr. and Mrs. Benedict Calvert), who are at hand and competent to give it, are at the same time the most proper to be consulted in so interesting an event. For my own part, I never did, nor do I believe I ever shall, give advice to a woman who is setting out on a matrimonial voyage; first, because I never could advise one to marry without her own consent; and, secondly, because I know it is to no purpose to advise her to refrain, when she has obtained it. A woman very rarely asks an opinion or requires advice on such an occasion till

her resolution is formed; and then it is with the hope
and expectation of obtaining a sanction—not that she
means to be governed by your disapprobation, that she
applies. In a word, the plain English of the application
may be summed up in these words: 'I wish you to think
as I do; but if, unhappily you differ from me in opinion,
my heart I must confess is fixed, and I have gone too
far now to retract.'

"If Mrs. Custis should ever suggest anything of this
kind to me, I will give her my opinion of the *measure,*
not of the *man,* with candor, and to the following effect:
'I never expected you would spend the rest of your days
in widowhood; but in a matter so important, and so interesting to yourself, children, and connections, I wish
you would make a prudent choice. To do which, many
considerations are necessary: such as the family connections of the man, his fortune (which is not the *most*
essential in my eye), the line of conduct he has observed,
and the disposition and frame of his mind. You should
consider what prospect there is of his proving kind and
affectionate to you; just, generous, and attentive to your
children; and how far his connections will be agreeable
to you; for when they are once formed, agreeable or
not, the die being cast, your fate is fixed."

Mrs. Custis married Dr. Stuart soon afterwards, and
the doctor proved able to withstand all the tests by which
Washington could measure him. He became a trusted
friend.

When the second Nelly Custis "wanted and deserved
a good husband," Washington was well pleased with her
selection of his favorite nephew, Lawrence Lewis. The

young people were married on the General's birthday, February 22, 1799. It was the wish of the young bride that Washington should wear to her wedding the splendid new embroidered uniform which had been designed for him by the board of general officers. He wore, instead, the plain continental buff and blue, in which he felt at home. The magnificent white plumes which General Pinckney had given him to wear in the hat of the uniform, Washington gave to the bride, as he himself had no desire to wear such finery. The young couple continued to live at Mount Vernon, to the great joy of Washington, who loved them both.

Washington at this time systematically occupied himself in putting his earthly affairs in order. To Mr. McHenry he wrote in March: "Being the executor, the administrator, and trustee for others' estates, my greatest anxiety is to leave all these concerns in such a clear and distinct form that no reproach may attach itself to me when I shall have taken my departure for the land of spirits."

In April he surveyed, unassisted, and made a chart of some lands belonging to him near Alexandria, which he bequeathed to his adopted son, George Washington Parke Custis. "To complete this," he wrote, "employed nearly three days."

It is to Custis that we are indebted for a description of Washington in the last year of his life: "With all its developments of muscular power, the form of Washington had no appearance of bulkiness; and so harmonious were its proportions that he did not appear so passing tall as his portraits have represented. He was rather

"Mount Vernon, 20th September, 1799

"Dear Sir: From the moment Mrs. Washington and
~self adopted the two youngest children of the late Mr.
.stis, it became my intention (if they survived me, and
iducted themselves to my satisfaction) to consider
m in my will when I was about to make a distribu-
n of my property. This determination has undergone
diminution, but is strengthened by the connection one
them has formed with my family.

"The expense at which I live, and the unproductive-
s of my estate, will not allow me to lessen my income
ile I remain in my present situation. On the contrary,
·e it not for occasional supplies of money in payment
lands sold within the last four or five years, to the
ount of upward of fifty thousand dollars, I should not
able to support the former without involving myself
lebt and difficulties.

"But as it has been understood, from expressions oc-
onally dropped from Nelly Custis, now your wife,
t it is the wish of you both to settle in this neighbor-
d, contiguous to her friends, and as it would be in-
edient as well as expensive for you to make a purse of land, when a measure which is in contemplation
ild place you on more eligible ground, I shall inform
that, in the will which I have made, which I have
ne, and have no disposition to alter, that the part of
Mount Vernon tract which lies north of the public
l leading from the Gum Spring to Colchester, con-
ing two thousand acres, with the Dogue-River farm,
, and distillery, I have left you. Gray's Heights is

spare than full during his whole life; this is readily ascer-
tained from his weight. The last time he weighed was
in the summer of 1799, when, having made the tour of his
farms, accompanied by an English gentleman, he called
at his mill and was weighed. The writer placed the
weight in the scales. The Englishman, not so tall, but
stout, square built, and fleshy, weighed heavily, and expressed much surprise that the General had not out-
weighed him, when Washington observed that the best
weight of his best days never exceeded from two hundred and ten to two hundred and twenty pounds. In
the instance alluded to he weighed a little rising two
hundred and ten. In the prime of life Washington stood
six feet two inches, and measured precisely six feet when
attired for the grave.

"The power of Washington's arm was displayed when
the late and venerable Charles Wilson Peale was one
day at Mount Vernon, in 1772, engaged in painting the
portrait of the provincial colonel. Some young men were
pitching the bar. Washington looked on for a time;
then grasping the missile in his master-hand, he whirled
the iron through the air far, very far, beyond any of its
former limits . . . Up to his sixty-eighth year he mounted
a horse with surprising agility, and rode with the ease
and gracefulness of his better days."

Custis, in directing a visitor whom he met on the
Mount Vernon grounds, gave a delightful description
of the retired General. "You will meet, sir," said young
Custis, "with an old gentleman riding alone, in plain
drab clothes, a broad-brimmed white hat, a hickory
switch in his hand, and carrying an umbrella with a

long staff which is attached to his saddle-bow. That person, sir, is General Washington." The visitor, a Revolutionary aid-de-camp, Richard Kidder Meade, smilingly replied that he believed he should recognize the general upon encountering him.

In July Washington wrote and executed his last will and testament. It was written entirely by himself; and at the bottom of each page of the manuscript he signed his name in full—George Washington.

A paragraph in his will answers the question which has sometimes been asked, in a critical spirit, "Why did not Washington manumit his slaves during his lifetime?" He was for many years anxious to give them freedom, to see the system abolished from America. In 1783 he had written to Lafayette: "The scheme which you propose, to encourage the emancipation of the black people in this country, from the state of bondage in which they are held, is a striking evidence of the benevolence of your heart. I shall be happy to join you in so laudable a work."

To Robert Morris he wrote in October, 1786: "There is not a man living who wishes more sincerely than I do to see a plan adopted for the abolition of slavery; but there is only one proper and effectual mode by which it can be accomplished, and that is by legislative authority; and this, as far as my suffrage will go, shall never be wanting. But when slaves, who are happy and contented with their present masters, are tampered with and seduced to leave them; when masters are taken unawares by these practices; when a conduct of this kind begets

discontent on one side and resentment when it happens to fall on a man who measure with that of the Society (Q loses his property for want of means t oppressive in such a case and not hum cause it introduces more evils than it ca

To John F. Mercer, of Virginia, months later: "I never mean, unless so cumstances should compel me to it, to slave by purchase, it being among my f some plan adopted by which slavery in be abolished by law."

In 1794 he wrote to Tobias Lear, tary, then in England, endeavoring to of some of Washington's wild lands, th had in view in making sales was to pl position to emancipate his slaves. "Ano wrote—"which is, indeed, more power rest—is, to liberate a certain species of p possess very reluctantly to my own feel imperious necessity compels," etc.

In 1797 he wrote to his nephew, L "I wish, from my soul, that the legislat could see the policy of a gradual abolitic might prevent much future mischief."

Some time later Lawrence Lewis, wh was still living at Mount Vernon, ap ington for a portion of his estate. Lewi visit with his friends at Fredericksburg, a wrote to him as follows:

bequeathed to you and her jointly, if you incline to build
on it, and few better sites for a house than Gray's Hill
and that range are to be found in this country or elsewhere.

"You may also have what is properly Dogue-Run
farm, the mill, and distillery, on a just and equitable rent;
as also the lands belonging thereto, on a reasonable hire,
either next year, or the year following—it being necessary, in my opinion, that a young man should have objects of employment. Idleness is disreputable under any
circumstances; productive of no good, even when unac-
companied by vicious habits; and you might commence
building as soon as you please, during the progress of
which Mount Vernon might be made your home.

"You may conceive that building before you have an
absolute title to the land is hazardous. To obviate this,
I shall only remark that it is not likely any occurrence
will happen, or any change take place, that would alter
my present intention (if the conduct of yourself and wife
is such as to merit a continuance of it); but be this as it
may, that you may proceed on sure ground with respect
to the buildings, I will agree and this letter shall be an
evidence of it—that if hereafter I should find cause to
make any other disposition of the property *here* mentioned, I will pay the actual cost of such buildings to
you or yours.

"Although I have not the most distant idea that any
event will happen that could effect a change in my present
determination, nor any suspicions that you or Nelly could
conduct yourselves in such a manner as to incur my seri-

ous displeasure, yet, at the same time that I am inclined to do justice to others, it behooves me to take care of myself, by keeping the staff in my own hands.

"That you may have a more perfect idea of the landed property I have bequeathed to you and Nelly in my will, I transmit a plan of it, every part of which is correctly laid down and accurately measured, showing the number of fields, lots, meadows, etc., with the contents and relative situation of each; all of which, except the mill and swamp, which has never been considered as a part of Dogue-Run farm, and is retained merely for the purpose of putting it into a better state of improvement, you may have on the terms beforementioned.

"With every kind wish for you and Nelly, in which your aunt, who is still much indisposed, unites, I remain, your affectionate uncle,

"Geo. Washington."

As the year 1799 was drawing toward its close, the family circle included the general and Mrs. Washington, Lawrence and Nelly Lewis, and her brother, young Custis. Colonel Tobias Lear resided in the home as the secretary and beloved friend of the General.

Washington, as winter approached, continued the usual rounds of his farms, undeterred by frost or storm. He was in the full enjoyment of health and strength, and in a tranquil state of mind. To the young men of his family Washington disclosed all his plans for further improvement of his estate. One of his projects was a new family burial-vault. He showed young Lewis the spot he had in mind for it, and the form and dimensions in which he purposed to build it, saying, "This change I shall make the first of all, for I may require it before the rest."

Lewis in later years told of his last farewell to his uncle, made in the firm conviction of their early reunion, saying, "When I parted from him, he stood on the steps of the front door, where he took leave of myself and another. He had taken his usual ride, and the clear, healthy flush on his cheek, and his sprightly manner brought the remark from both of us that we had never seen the General look so well. I have sometimes thought him decidedly the handsomest man I ever saw; and, when in a lively mood, so full of pleasantry, so agreeable to all with whom he associated, I could hardly realize that he was the same Washington whose dignity awed all who approached him."

CHAPTER XVII

THE LAST HOURS OF WASHINGTON

The title is that of Custis, whose affectionate interpretation of those hours is preferred to the account of Colonel Lear, although it was Lear who gave to Washington's last hours the comfort of loving companionship and ministration.

To read of the death of Washington as recorded by Lear is like reading a chapter from a dusty, mildewed, medical report. Colonel Lear noted in his Diary every detail of the futile measures resorted to by the family and their medical advisers to prolong the life of Washington. The entries reveal the limitations of medical knowledge of the day.

Custis was not present at the bedside of the man who had stood in the place of a father to him from infancy. The fact that he was absent from the home circle bears witness to the unexpectedness of the General's illness. He had gone with Lawrence Lewis to New Kent, probably on some errand connected with the administration of the Custis property there. Where Custis is mistaken in detail, we turn to Lear for verity.

"On the morning of the thirteenth" (December, 1799), says Custis, "the General was making some improvements in the front of Mount Vernon. As was usual with him, he carried his own compass, noted his observations, and marked out the ground. The day became rainy, with sleet; and the improver remained so long exposed to the inclemency of the weather as to be considerably wetted before his return to the house. About one o'clock he was seized with chilliness and nausea, but having changed his clothes, he sat down to his indoor work—there being no moment of his time for which he had not provided an appropriate employment.

"At night on joining his family circle, the General complained of a slight indisposition, and after a single cup of tea, repaired to his library."

Lear records: "He sat in the parlor with Mrs. Washington and myself reading, till about nine o'clock, when Mrs. Washington went up into Mrs. Lewis' room, and left the General and myself reading the papers. He was very cheerful, and when he met with anything interesting or entertaining, he read it aloud as well as his hoarseness would permit. He requested me to read to him the Debates of the Virginia Assembly, on the election of a senator and governor; and, on hearing Mr. Madison's observations respecting Mr. Monroe, he appeared much affected, and spoke with some degree of asperity on the subject, which I endeavored to moderate, as I always did on such occasions. On his retiring, I observed to him that he had better take something to remove his cold. He answered, 'No, you know I never take anything for a cold. Let it go as it came.'"

As Custis had the account of the night from his grandmother, we revert here to his narrative: "Mrs. Washington retired about the usual family hours, but becoming alarmed at not hearing the accustomed sound of the library door as it closed for the night, she rose again, and continued sitting up, in much anxiety and suspense. At length the well-known step was heard on the stair, and upon the General's entering his chamber, the lady chided him for staying up so late, knowing him to be unwell.

"Having first covered the fire with care, the man of mighty labors sought repose; but it came not. . . . The night was passed in feverish restlessness and pain. It was only at daybreak he would consent that the overseer might be called in, and bleeding resorted to. A vein was opened, but no relief afforded. Couriers were dispatched to Dr. Craik, the family, and Drs. Dick and Brown, the consulting physicians, all of whom came with speed. The proper remedies were administered, but without producing their healing effects; while the patient, yielding to the anxious looks of all around him, waived his usual objections to medicines, and took those which were prescribed without hesitation or remark. The medical gentlemen spared not their skill, and all the resources of their art were exhausted in unwearied endeavors to preserve this noblest work of nature.

"The night approached—the last night of Washington. The weather became severely cold while the group gathered nearer to the couch of the sufferer, watching with intense anxiety for the slightest dawning of hope. He spoke but little. To the respectful and affectionate inquiries of an old family servant, as she smoothed down his pillow, how he felt himself, he answered, 'I am very ill.' To Mrs. Washington he said, 'Go to my desk, and in the private drawer you will find two papers—bring them to me.' They were brought. He continued, 'These are my wills; preserve this one and burn the other,' which was accordingly done."

At this point Lear tells of returning to the General's bedside and taking his hand. "He said to me, 'I find I am going. My breath cannot last long. I believed from the first that the disorder would prove fatal. Do you arrange and record all my late military letters and papers. Arrange my accounts and settle my books, as you know more about them than anyone else, and let Mr. Rawlins finish recording my other letters, which he has begun.' I told him this should be done. He then asked if I recollected anything which it was essential for him to do, as he had but a very short time to continue with us. I told him that I could recollect nothing, but that I hoped he was not so near his end. He observed, smiling, that he certainly was, and that, as it was the debt which we must all pay, he looked to the event with perfect resignation.

"In the course of the afternoon he appeared to be in great pain and distress, from the difficulty of breathing, and frequently changed his posture in the bed. On these occasions I lay upon the bed and endeavored to raise him and turn him with as much ease as possible. He appeared penetrated with gratitude for my attentions, and often said, 'I am afraid I shall fatigue you too much,' and, upon my assuring him that I could feel nothing but a wish to give him ease, he replied, 'Well, it is a debt we must pay to each other, and I hope, when you want aid of this kind, you will find it.'

"He asked when Mr. Lewis and Washington Custis

would return. (They were then in New Kent.) I told him, about the twentieth of the month. . . .

"About five o'clock Dr. Craik came again into the room, and upon going to the bedside the General said to him, 'Doctor, I die hard, but I am not afraid to go. I believed from my first attack, that I should not survive it. My breath cannot last long.' The doctor pressed his hand, but could not utter a word. He retired from the bedside, and sat by the fire absorbed in grief. . . .

"About ten o'clock he (Washington) made several attempts to speak to me before he could effect it. At length he said, 'I am just going. Have me decently buried; and do not let my body be put into the vault in less than three days after I am dead.' I bowed assent, for I could not speak. He then looked at me again and said, 'Do you understand me?' I replied, 'Yes.' ' 'Tis well,' said he.

"About ten minutes before he expired (which was between ten and eleven o'clock) his breathing became easier. He lay quietly; he withdrew his hand from mine, felt his own pulse. I saw his countenance change. I spoke to Dr. Craik, who sat by the fire. He came to the bedside. The General's hand fell from his wrist. I took it in mine, and pressed it to my bosom. Dr. Craik put his hands over his eyes. Washington expired without a struggle or a sigh.

"While we were fixed in silent grief, Mrs. Washington, who was sitting at the foot of the bed, asked with a firm and collected voice, 'Is he gone?' I could not speak, but held up my hand as a signal that he was no more. 'Tis well,' said she, in the same voice. 'All is now over; I shall soon follow him; I have no more trials to pass through.' "

The closing paragraph is quoted from Custis.

"It may be asked, why was the ministry of religion wanting to shed its peaceful and benign luster upon the last hours of Washington? Why was he, to whom the observance of sacred things were ever primary duties throughout life, without their consolations in his last moments? We answer, circumstances did not permit. It was but for a little while that the disease assumed so threatening a character as to forbid the encouragement of hope; yet, to stay that summons which none may refuse, to give still farther length of days to him whose time-honored life was so dear to mankind, prayer was not wanting to the throne of Grace. Close to the couch of the sufferer, resting her head upon that ancient book, with which she had been wont to hold pious communion a portion of every day, for more than half a century, was the venerable consort, absorbed in silent prayer, and from which she only arose when the mourning group prepared to lead her from the chamber of the dead.

"Such were the last hours of Washington."

CHAPTER XVIII

ESTIMATES OF WASHINGTON

The news of the death of Washington created a profound sensation throughout Europe as well as in Great Britain. Napoleon Bonaparte, then First Consul of France, announced the death to the French army with the order that all flags and standards of the French service should be draped with black crêpe for ten days.

Lord Bridport, commander of a British fleet at Torbay, on the coast of Devon, ordered the flags of all ships under his command at half-mast.

The Marquis de Chastellux, who had shared with Washington the anxieties of the siege of Yorktown, said of him: "Let it be repeated that Condé was intrepid, Luzerne was prudent, Eugène was adroit, Catinat was disinterested. It is not thus that Washington will be characterized. It will be said of him, *at the end of a long civil war he had nothing to reproach himself.* . . . He was brave without temerity, laborious without ambition, generous without prodigality, noble without pride, virtuous without severity."

Washington, before his death, had received many tributes from the great of the earth.* Count Herzburg wrote to him from Berlin, "I have always admired your great virtues and qualities, your disinterested patri-

---

* Most of the tributes here given are taken from the writings of foreigners.

otism, your unshaken courage and simplicity of manner—
qualifications by which you surpass men even the most
celebrated of antiquity."

Frederick the Great, of Prussia, is said to have characterized Washington's military operations between the
twenty-fifth of December, 1776, and the fourth of January,
1777, as the most brilliant of ancient or modern times
within his knowledge. His portrait, sent to Washington
inscribed, "From the oldest general in the world to the
greatest," was treasured at Mount Vernon.

Lord Erskine, Lord Chancellor of Great Britain, had
written to General Washington, "You are the only being
for whom I have an awful reverence."

Perhaps the tribute most prized by Washington in his
later years was that of his old friend and compatriot,
Benjamin Franklin, who, in his will, made this bequest:
"My fine crab-tree walking-stick, with a gold head curiously wrought in the form of a cap of Liberty, I give to
my friend, and the friend of mankind, George Washington. If it were a scepter, he has merited it and would
become it." Washington in his turn bequeathed this cane
to his brother Charles.

John Marshall, who for many years had scrutinized
Washington's every public act with the keenest interest,
said of him, "In his civil administration, as in his military
career, ample and repeated proofs were exhibited of that
practical good sense, of that sound judgment, which is
perhaps the most rare and is certainly the most valuable
quality of the human mind."

Lord Byron, in his poem "Ode to Napoleon" apostro-
phizes Washington in the following stanza:

Where may the wearied eye repose
    When gazing on the great,
Where neither guilty glory glows
    Nor despicable State!
Yes, One—the first, the last, the best,
The Cincinnatus of the West,
    Whom Envy dared not hate—
Bequeathed the name of Washington
To make men blush there was but One!

A writer in the *Encyclopedia Britannica* expressed the opinion, "Of all men that ever lived, he was the greatest of good men and the best of great men."

As late as 1860 Lord Brougham, upon his installation as chancellor of the University of Edinburgh, having spoken of Napoleon and Wellington, said, "But in Washington we may contemplate every excellence, military and civil, applied to the service of his country and of mankind —a triumphant warrior, unshaken in confidence when the most sanguine had a right to despair; a successful ruler in all the difficulties of a course wholly untried— directing the formation of a new government for a great people, the first time so vast an experiment had ever been tried by man; voluntarily and unostentatiously retiring from supreme power with the veneration of all parties, of all nations, of all mankind, that the rights of men may be conserved, and that his example might never be appealed to by vulgar tyrants. It will be the duty of the historian and the sage, in all ages, to omit no occasion of commemorating this illustrious man; and until time shall be no more, will a test of the progress which our race has